WESTERN
SAHARA

INTERNATIONAL PEACE ACADEMY
OCCASIONAL PAPER SERIES

WESTERN SAHARA

Anatomy of a Stalemate

Erik Jensen

LYNNE
RIENNER
PUBLISHERS

BOULDER
LONDON

Published in the United States of America in 2005 by
Lynne Rienner Publishers, Inc.
1800 30th Street, Boulder, Colorado 80301
www.rienner.com

and in the United Kingdom by
Lynne Rienner Publishers, Inc.
3 Henrietta Street, Covent Garden, London WC2E 8LU

Library of Congress Cataloging-in-Publication Data
Jensen, Erik.
    Western Sahara : anatomy of a stalemate / Erik Jensen.
    p.   cm. — (An International Peace Academy occasional paper)
    Includes bibliographical references and index.
    ISBN 1-58826-305-3 (pbk. : alk. paper)
    1. Western Sahara. 2. Western Sahara—Politics and government—1975–
3. United Nations—Western Sahara. I. Title. II. Series: International Peace
Academy occasional paper series.
DT346.S7J47 2004
964.8'03—dc22   2004015449

British Cataloguing in Publication Data
A Cataloguing in Publication record for this book
is available from the British Library.

Printed and bound in the United States of America

        The paper used in this publication meets the requirements
  ∞   of the American National Standard for Permanence of
        Paper for Printed Library Materials Z39.48-1992.

    5 4 3 2 1

*To all who work for a just and
peaceful future in Western Sahara
and in memory of those
who have given their lives*

Contents

Foreword

David M. Malone,
President, International Peace Academy

It is with great pleasure that the International Peace Academy (IPA) presents this book that traces the history of the efforts undertaken to determine the sovereignty of Western Sahara. The issue of Western Sahara, which has been largely underaddressed by the policymaking and academic communities, qualifies as one of the most intractable issues of state formation and democratization in North Africa. Despite years of involvement by the United Nations and, before that, the Organization of African Unity, Western Sahara's status, as either an independent state or as part of Morocco, remains undecided.

In this book, Erik Jensen, who served as head of the United Nations Mission for the Referendum in Western Sahara (MINURSO) from 1994 to 1998, expertly details the major issues that have characterized the ebb and flow of the referendum process in Western Sahara. He focuses specifically on the problems encountered by the UN, the region's governments—Morocco in particular—and the inhabitants of Western Sahara by identifying those eligible to decide the status of Western Sahara. From his unique perspective and intimate knowledge of the region, Jensen presents a balanced narrative from the point of view of all the actors and provides a rich historical, political, and social context for understanding the impasses of the referendum process. In addition to identifying local obstacles, Jensen highlights how international and regional concerns impacted the process.

The IPA Africa Program prides itself on bringing interesting issues and fresh perspectives to the fore for policymakers and academics, but these achievements could not have been possible without the support of its donors. In particular, the IPA would like to thank the governments of Denmark, Finland, Germany, the Netherlands, Norway, and Sweden, as well as the United Kingdom's Department for International Development, Canada's Department of Foreign Affairs and International Trade, the Rockefeller Foundation, the William and Flora Hewlett Foundation, and the Ford Foundation. Their support of the Africa Program has allowed scholars to under-take important original research on subjects, like Western Sahara, that do not necessarily receive the attention from policymakers that they need.

Useful to policymakers, civil society organizations, and academics, Jensen's book provides a treasure trove of behind-the-scenes lessons on conflict mediation. It is particularly instructive on the role of international organizations, neighboring states, and rules of engagement. We hope readers will find this publication to be a unique contribution to the practice and literature on negotiation and conflict resolution.

Preface

I am grateful to the International Peace Academy for asking me to write this occasional paper; without such urging, it would not have been done. In particular, I would like to thank Adekeye Adebajo, who promoted the idea, and Dorina Bekoe, who helped bring it to fruition.

The focus of the book is on *identification*. However mysterious—and tedious—the identification procedure seemed to many, it was at the core of the United Nations settlement plan for Western Sahara. It also has been the most divisive issue, intended to establish the determining "self" in a choice between integration with Morocco and independence.

It was a great privilege to work in Western Sahara for five years, and for four of those as head of mission. MINURSO was charged with keeping the peace—not one of the few, sad fatalities in that period was due to hostile fire—in a sensitive and important part of the world where great armies were deployed over a vast area, while endeavoring to move the two sides closer to resolving the dispute. Implementing the rest of a flawed settlement plan was another matter. As some foresaw, it would never be accomplished on the basis of purely voluntary cooperation. Almost every step became contentious. Gaining and retaining the confidence of the opposing parties was an unrelenting challenge, as my predecessors found. I am proud that at the end of a prolonged mission, both the Frente Polisario and Morocco were more than generous in expressing their respect. But it is profoundly disappointing that after all our efforts the conflict is far from resolved. Nevertheless, no one can fail to be moved by conditions in the bleak, rocky desert camps where thousands of refugee families have lived for so long.

Daunting as our common task often seemed, it was wonderfully rewarding to work with committed, dedicated people. I wish to thank all the MINURSO staff who were with me during those exciting and frustrating years: members of my immediate office, especially Halima and Paulette; the force

11

commanders and military observers; the police commissioner and Civpol; the Identification Commission; the chief administrative officer, a good friend in difficult times, and his staff; as well as those like Mohammed Aouad, who aided me personally in multiple ways. Two individuals who were not in Western Sahara had a critical role as desk officers in New York: I would like to pay fulsome tribute to Louise Laheurte and Anna Theophilopoulou for their splendid support as colleagues and for their friendship; Louise was also unstinting in giving me the benefit of her background knowledge, insight, and critical judgment while I was working on this book.

Finally, I wish to express my appreciation to the London School of Economics and Political Science for awarding me a visiting fellowship at the Centre for International Studies. It proved immensely helpful during both the research and writing stages of the project.

—Erik Jensen

1

Western Sahara: Independence or Integration with Morocco?

The referendum planned for Western Sahara resembles a desert mirage. The elusive issue: who is a Sahrawi, who is a Western Saharan, and who should be entitled to vote?[1] Who should be the determining self in the act of self-determination?

The United Nations (UN), Security Council, and Secretariat have been criticized,[2] even accused of incompetence, for the failure of the United Nations Mission for the Referendum in Western Sahara (MINURSO) to implement the settlement plan supposedly agreed by the Kingdom of Morocco and the Algerian-backed Frente Polisario (Frente Popular para la Liberacion de Seguia el-Hamra y Rio de Oro), as parties to the conflict.[3] In reality, the two agreed to differing and incompatible interpretations of what was proposed. Yet the Security Council, speaking for the international community, endorsed the proposal in 1990 and 1991 and welcomed the detailed criteria on the premise of willing cooperation by the parties.

Morocco and the Frente Polisario have been consistent in their attitudes and steadfast in upholding them. The core issue was and remains the electorate deemed qualified to vote in a referendum. For Morocco the right to vote had to be comprehensively based on the principle of jus sanguinis, extending to all Saharan tribes linked to the former Spanish Sahara; for the Polisario it should be narrowly defined, mainly according to jus soli, but in effect largely limited to those counted in the Spanish census of 1974. These were positions that they considered closed to compromise. The consequences of one interpretation or the other's prevailing are recognized by both as determinant in a winner-take-all referendum, with the unnuanced choice between integration with Morocco and independence under Polisario.

That the settlement plan was adopted with so basic a flaw apparent to the principal architects may be due to their belief that a politically realistic compromise would be negotiated, and the negotiated compromise endorsed in a referendum, thus completing the process of self-determination. From 1992,

Western Sahara lies on the northwest African coast immediately to the south of Morocco, north and west of Mauritania and southwest of Algeria. The population is currently estimated at around 300,000, living in a desert exceeding Great Britain in area. The coastal waters offer rich fishing, and high-quality phosphate is extracted; there is speculation about other mineral deposits.

From 1884 to 1975, the territory was a Spanish colony, although it was only in the final decades that Spain exercised administrative control over the Sahrawi tribes in the interior. When Spain agreed to relinquish colonial power, Morocco and Mauritania approached the World Court for an advisory opinion, which they then interpreted as supporting their historical claims to the territory, and took control. The Polisario independence movement, with Algerian, Libyan, and other support, political and military, launched offensives against Morocco and Mauritania. Mauritania relinquished its share of Western Sahara, which was occupied by Morocco.

Morocco was able to secure possession by constructing a 2,000-kilometer defensive wall, though military activity continued. In 1990–1991 the UN Security Council approved a settlement plan leading to a referendum when voters would opt for either independence or integration with Morocco. An informal cease-fire became formal after a renewed bout of fighting. The problem remained to establish an electoral roll; the two sides had incompatible views as to who should vote.

UN Secretary-General Boutros Boutros-Ghali in periodic reports to the Security Council[4] suggested considering alternatives to the plan. Attempts to organize contact between the parties and talks, as urged by both the Organization of African Unity (OAU)—recently renamed the African Union (AU)—and the UN General Assembly, had first to surmount Morocco's reluctance to regard the Frente Polisario as the "other party" to the conflict, rather than Algeria. Morocco refused to accord the front any political recognition. It then responded to Polisario's eagerness to negotiate by presenting pro-Moroccan Saharans as interlocutors. The implication that this was a dispute between Saharans, thus domestic and not an international issue, exasperated the Polisario, and after the failure of serious efforts in July and October 1993 and again in January 1994, confidence in the usefulness of talks was relegated to the wings to await more propitious timing.

Prospects for the settlement plan fared marginally better. Though few expected it could be made to work, it was the only official mandate. The detailed criteria for identifying potential voters, presented by UN Secretary-General Javier Perez de Cuellar on the eve of his departure and tepidly "welcomed" by the Security Council, appeared to favor Morocco and were at first rejected by the Polisario. Morocco may well have been anticipating that Polisario would cry foul and opt out of the plan. It took all by surprise in the spring of 1994 when the Polisario was persuaded, albeit grudgingly, to embark on identification in accordance with the criteria. Given what appeared to be insurmountable obstacles to completing the process—the absence of surviving tribal leaders for fully one-third of the undisputed eighty-eight tribal subgroups and Polisario's rejection of most, if not all, applicants from three tribal groupings (out of ten tribes and tribal group-ings)—the launch of identification could best be regarded as a means of locking Morocco and the Frente Polisario into regular and nonviolent inter-action, fostering a change of attitude that might eventually permit con-structive negotiation.

The premise of cooperation by the parties made for heavy going. Both sides sought to control the process of identification so as to achieve maxi-mum compliance with their concept of the electoral roll. Morocco, confi-dent that time and circumstance worked in its favor, had little incentive to overcome obstacles as these arose, and Polisario, albeit for quite different reasons, also believed time to be on its side. In identification, Polisario's emphasis on the Spanish census of 1974 as the only valid basis for defining the electorate was to its advantage: names had been recorded and recog-nized documents were available. Candidates not among the 72,370 included by name in the revised census list—and a total of 233,487 applications were received, predominantly on the Moroccan side—relied on oral testi-mony to substantiate their claim to be considered Saharans originating in the territory. This made a harder case for Morocco.

The identification procedure was without precedent. The formula that was developed and agreed to provided for observers from both parties and the OAU to be constantly present, and a key role for tribal leaders (shaikhs): one tribal leader, belonging to the tribal subgroup being identified, from each side. The tribal leaders, under quranic oath, were expected to confirm the applicants' personal identity and, for all those not included in the re-vised census listing, their claim to membership in an accepted tribal group and Saharan paternity. When tribal leaders concurred, this posed no prob-lem, but the Identification Commission faced a quandary when the evi-dence of one shaikh conflicted with that of another and no acceptable sup-porting documentation was available. In so highly charged a situation, it was not surprising that it became evident that the tribal leaders were being politicized. The vote of one could, in effect, be used to veto the other in every case dependent on oral testimony.

In spite of these difficulties and despite interruptions, the identification procedure proved its worth initially. Agreement was even reached on alternate tribal leaders to replace most of those elected in 1973 but no longer living, and a range of incidental and practical problems were resolved. But there was no compromise on three tribal groupings that the Polisario refused to recognize as constituting authentic Western Saharan tribes and without which Morocco refused to proceed. In late 1995, identification stalled. By then a total of 77,058 applicants had been processed and convoked, exceeding the number in the revised list and the census, and 60,112 had come forward and been formally identified.

The interruption of the process prompted a new tack in negotiation, and after an uncertain start, the parties agreed to meet together in 1996. Morocco stipulated that talks be in secret and not be exploited for any publicity; the Polisario's main condition was that its representatives deal with the Moroccan king or the crown prince. It was possible to compromise on some of the other conditions posed. An exploratory encounter in Geneva exceeded expectations, and in September in Rabat, an important Polisario delegation met with the crown prince, who was advised by the powerful and knowledgeable Moroccan minister of interior, Driss Basri. The first round focused successfully on the agenda as it was understood. It may have moved too well and too fast for others who were interested, and in the face of vested interests. No immediate meeting with the king followed, as tentatively foreseen, but the talks concluded on a positive note with agreement to resume in the very near future.

Unfortunately, this most promising development coincided with the U.S. presidential election and Boutros-Ghali's aspiration to seek another term as UN Secretary-General. Influential U.S. politicians, campaigning to oust Boutros-Ghali, had no reason to be supportive of a UN initiative, and Boutros-Ghali was preoccupied with being reelected. Once aware of developments in New York and Washington, both Morocco and the Frente Polisario preferred to await the election of someone "more favorable to its position."

One of the first acts of Kofi Annan on becoming Secretary-General in December 1996 was to appoint former U.S. secretary of state James A. Baker III as his personal envoy for Western Sahara. Baker's mandate was to see whether the settlement plan could be implemented as it stood or could be implemented with agreed changes, or if there was a third way forward. The assumption was that Baker, with evident U.S. backing, would nudge the parties toward a negotiated compromise.

As it transpired, both Morocco and Polisario claimed that they wanted to stay with the plan—on their terms. Through a series of encounters, Baker negotiated the Houston accords, which permitted resumption of the settlement plan. Whether restarting identification was helpful is open to question. It increased the cost of the mission and prolonged the agony. Given earlier experience, the tribal leaders were almost certain to serve political ends, which would undermine Moroccan hopes for the large number of applicants from the contested groups, the vast majority of whom depended on oral testimony. That both sides were informed of the results of identification hardened positions further. Morocco became increasingly and openly critical of a process inimical to its interests, and Polisario ever less disposed to accept any alternative.

The resurrected process led to the inevitable conclusion. The Polisario resisted for as long as possible the identification of those groups it considered non–Western Saharan and for which it had no shaikh. Morocco insisted on their identification. When the results of all other identification to date were released, those found ineligible appealed, leading to a dispute about grounds for appeal and how the appeals process should be conducted. A breakdown was averted by agreement to identify the contested groups, with the "most expert" persons available fulfilling the shaikhs' role, while at the same time proceeding to hear appeals. Appeals stayed blocked, though, and identification was doomed. Virtually all applicants from the contested groups depended on oral testimony, and virtually all were rejected. At the end, 195,589 persons had been identified, 86,412 were found eligible, and 131,038 appealed against exclusion or, in a few cases, questioned certain names of those included.[5] To have heard these appeals, on the basis of oral testimony provided by personal witnesses, would have been endless and was predestined to deliver an outcome unacceptable to one side or the other.

By 2001, Baker had concluded that the settlement plan would never be fully implemented with the parties' willing cooperation. He presented a "framework agreement" involving a two-stage process, which Morocco, after hesitation, accepted, but which was rejected by Polisario and Algeria.[6] Baker's subsequent attempt, in 2002, to have the Security Council choose one of four alternatives—the settlement plan, the framework agreement, partition of the territory, or closing the mission—which would then be imposed on the parties without further negotiation, failed to obtain the necessary support after long and heated discussion.[7] Instead, the Council asked the personal envoy to renew his efforts. In January 2003 Baker presented, in confidence, the "Peace Plan for Self-Determination of the People of Western Sahara" to Morocco, the Polisario, Algeria, and Mauritania and invited their comments. The plan made detailed provision for the exercise of power during a transitional period by an authority to be elected by returning refugees and persons included in a provisional voter list, but in addition permitted all who had resided in Western Sahara continuously since 30 December 1999 to vote in the conclusive act of self-determination. The Council was to have considered the reaction in March, but world events intervened. The full report appeared in May 2003,[8] and the Council decided to allow two more months to reflect on proposals, to which both sides objected, and which the Council was expected to impose. "Unlike the settlement plan, the peace plan does not require the consent of both parties at each and every step of its implementation."[9] The "interested parties" were asked to agree that the Secretary-General would have the authority to interpret the plan and that his interpretation would be binding.[10]

Polisario reacted negatively. Algeria was also critical. Morocco, albeit uncomfortable with many provisions, did not openly reject the plan. The Secretary-General, reporting to the Council, addressed what he saw as Morocco's main objection and suggested adding to the ballot a third choice offering self-government or autonomy.[11] He then presented the plan as "an optimum political solution"[12] and warned the Council against supporting a process subject to continuing negotiation with the parties.[13] As the Council was about to start deliberating, the Frente Polisario sprang an ingenious surprise by officially accepting the peace plan. Morocco, in a quandary, was obliged to articulate its opposition, above all rejecting any attempt to impose a settlement. The Council retreated to compromise: it expressed strong support for the Secretary-General's and Baker's efforts to achieve self-determination, while urging a political solution on the basis of agreement with the parties.[14] Subsequent efforts to induce Morocco to "engage in the process by accepting and implementing the plan"[15] met an angry response. Instead of an imposed plan, Morocco insisted on a mutually acceptable solution.[16]

During the autumn months of 2003, King Mohammed VI was reported to have been reassured by President George W. Bush while in New York for the General Assembly, and by U.S. assistant secretary of state William Burns, who visited Rabat. President Jacques Chirac of France, on a state visit to Morocco, was explicit in affirming that the position of France in this affair consisted in supporting the position of Morocco, and he did not believe that a solution could be imposed by the international community against the will of one of the parties.[17]

Notes

1. Saharan and Sahrawi are used interchangeably without political or other connotation.
2. See, for example, Adekeye Adebajo, "Selling Out the Sahara: The Tragic Tale of the UN Referendum," Cornell University, Institute for African Development, Occasional Papers Series, Spring 2002, 36.
3. The mission is generally known by the French acronym MINURSO, derived from Mission des Nations Unies pour l'organisation d'un referendum au Sahara Occidental.

4. Reports of the Secretary-General to the Security Council on the situation of Western Sahara: S/23662 (28 February 1992), par. 30; S/24040 (29 May 1992), par. 11; S/25170 (26 January 1993), par. 32.

5. Report of the Secretary-General, S/2001/148 (20 February 2001), Annex I.

6. Report of the Secretary-General, S/2001/613 (20 June 2001), Annex I.

7. Report of the Secretary-General, S/2002/178 (19 February 2002), par. 47 seq.

8. Report of the Secretary-General, S/2003/565 (23 May 2003).

9. Ibid., par. 49.

10. Ibid., Annex II, par. 22.

11. Ibid., par. 53.

12. Ibid., par. 50.

13. Ibid., par. 56.

14. Security Council Resolution S/RES/1495 (2003), 31 July 2003.

15. Report of the Secretary-General, S/2003/1016 (16 October 2003), par. 27.

16. Document S/2003/1028 (21 October 2003).

17. Press conference, 11 October 2003, L'Elysee website, www.elysee.fr.

Northwest Africa
Showing Spanish Possessions and Protectorate, circa 1950

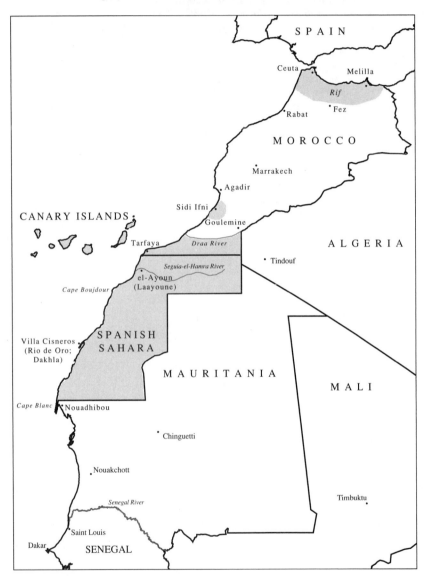

2

People, Place, and the Role of Spain

The geography and the history of Western Sahara have direct bearing on the dispute.[1] Until the discovery of phosphate rock at Bou Craa, Western Sahara was not known for any proven mineral or other wealth. It is a vast, desolate area comparable in size to Great Britain (at 102,700 square miles) or the U.S. state of Colorado. Dramatic cliffs border the Atlantic coastline; shifting sand dunes give way farther inland to mountainous outcrops and the inhospitable expanse of *hammada,* the rocky desert of the interior plateau. Vegetation is extremely sparse, to say the least, with *Acacia radiana* as almost the only tree and a few palms in modest oases. Rainfall is minimal, rarely exceeding 5 centimeters in a year. Furious sandstorms are common. There are four seasons, as one old Sahrawi explained: the season of extreme heat, the season of freezing cold nights, and, less calendar defined, the season of sandstorms and the season of flies.

It was not always so. Fossils show that parts of the region were under water in the remote past. Cave paintings and petroliths offer illuminating evidence of animal life in the savannah that prevailed from about 5000 to 2500 B.C. and of the Bafour people who lived there. Progressive desertification over centuries drove the giraffes, antelope, wild cattle, elephants, and rhinoceros to extinction and reduced human life to a nomadic existence dependent on the intermittent, meager grazing available. Tradition holds that the Bafour people gravitated southward, while, in the course of the first millennium B.C., Berber nomads began migrating into the territory from the north. The early Berbers to reach the Sahara were Sanhaja, one of the two main Berber groups of northwest Africa, and these came to dominate the region.

Islam was introduced during the eighth and ninth centuries. Toward the middle of the eleventh century a great leader, following a pilgrimage to Mecca, mounted a campaign, a holy war, to eliminate the superstitious beliefs and practices still prevailing. He was subsequently successful in mustering an army of followers, the Almoravid, which marched north, advancing into the Anti-Atlas ranges, and by 1059 reached the plains of northern Morocco. Yusuf ibn Tashfin founded Marrakech in 1062, before taking Fez in 1069 and with it completing the Almoravid conquest of Morocco. Ibn Tashfin went on to encompass Muslim Spain in his empire, but the ascendance of Christian Spain and tribal rivalry brought its collapse in the following century.

Power shifted over the years. Different dynasties achieved differing degrees of control over the tribes of the region. The Saadian dynasty had desert origins; in the mid-sixteenth century it successfully drove the Portuguese from what is now Agadir before advancing both north and south, as far as Timbuktu, to establish overall ascendancy under Ahmed el-Mansour. In the seventeenth century the first Alaouite sultan, from southeastern Morocco and close to the caravan world, entered Fez and Marrakech and expanded into the Sahara. His successor, Moulay Ismail, consolidated control of all Morocco and mounted a series of successful desert expeditions to achieve recognition of at least nominal sovereignty throughout the entire region. Effective power became intermittent in the decades that followed Moulay Ismail's death in 1727.

Arab Bedouin tribes had begun to invade the Maghreb in the eleventh century, and in the thirteenth century a Bedouin Arab people, the Maqil, penetrated the western Sahara. Over a period of time a group of tribes, known as Beni Hassan, purportedly originating in the Yemen, established themselves in the territory, mixing with and, in spite of sustained opposition, absorbing the earlier Sanhaja population.

The Beni Hassan were a warrior people with a marked hierarchy within the tribe and between tribes. Powerful tribes exacted payment "for protection" from those less powerful, who were obliged to pay tribute, although alliances and relative strength changed over time. Within the tribe the social stratification descended from warrior through artisan, craftsman, and bard to slave—black African slaves acquired through war and purchase. The Beni Hassan spoke Hassaniya, a characteristic dialect of Arabic that was closer to literary usage than the language spoken by others in the region, although it had also assimilated elements from the Berber. They dressed in their own fashion: men wore the *drah*—a voluminous outer garment, usually indigo blue, which accounts for their being called "the blue men"—and a turban; women wore the *malhaffah,* a length of lightweight colored material draped, and constantly redraped, about the body and over the head. They venerated a way of life adapted to the desert, as was their observance of Islam: they were zealous in devotion to prayer but washed with sand, not water, and it was exceedingly rare to encounter a Sahrawi who had completed the pilgrimage to Mecca; having no mosque buildings, they improvised an alignment of stones.

In constant search of pasturage for their camel herds and goats, they followed the clouds in hope of rainfall, becoming known as *les enfants des nuages* (the children of the clouds), and in so doing they roamed over thousands of miles. The camel, which is thought to have arrived from the east in the first century B.C., underpinned desert existence. This extraordinary animal was uniquely adapted to desert conditions. In extreme heat it could survive without drinking for five days, and in cooler weather for weeks on end. As a beast of burden it was capable of carrying great loads, 300 pounds or so, over vast distances. Its milk was an invaluable source of nourishment, protein rich and almost fat free; the female produced twelve pints a day, and up to twice as much after bearing young. Camel hair and hide served for tent cloth and leather, and its meat could be eaten when the occasion warranted. It made possible the trans-Saharan caravan trade that was to thrive for centuries.

There were no natural borders, apart from the sea at the Atlantic coastline. The wanderings of the Sahrawi tribes took them throughout Western Sahara and into what are now the countries of Mauritania, Algeria, and Morocco. To the south lay Chinguetti, eighth greatest city of the Islamic world, and Atar; to the northeast Tindouf; and to the north Goulemine, celebrated for its camel market. Western Sahara itself contained no great oases or prestigious settlements until the founding of Smara. It was like an ocean, a huge expanse to be traversed on the caravan routes from the port of one important trading center to another. Some caravaners, like sailors, even used a sextant.

The caravan trade carried ostrich plumes, gum, gold, ivory, and slaves from sub-Saharan Africa to markets farther north, whence the ostrich feathers and gum were shipped to Europe. On the return journey the camels were laden with European mass-produced fabric and tea, sugar, tobacco, and salt, the latter being an especially important commodity. The trade prospered until the late 1800s. The French capture of Timbuktu in 1894 enabled France to steer much business to the port of Saint Louis in Senegal. The Scot Donald Mackenzie had successfully established a trading counter at Tarfaya, at the northernmost edge of Western Sahara; when it closed in 1895, the whole region suffered.

European adventurers are recorded to have landed near Cape Boujdour as early as 1405, when they attacked a caravan there. More raids followed along the Saharan coast; there was also an attempt at peaceful barter. The Saharan tribesmen fiercely resisted any encroachment by foreigners, and the earliest European settlements were limited to peripheral, insecure toeholds on the coast. In 1476 the Spaniards reinforced their presence with a fort, which was besieged, relieved, and abandoned before Spain reasserted itself toward the end of the century. Santa Cruz, as the fort was known, was seized by Sahrawis in 1517 but was quickly retaken, only to be sacked in 1524 and this time given up for good. There was not to be another Spanish settlement on the Saharan coast until 1884.

Other European nations showed intermittent interest. The Portuguese had been off shore before the Spanish, who were followed by the French,

the English, and the Scots. The French chose for their base the island of
Arguin at Cape Blanc, near the dividing line between what was to become
Mauritania and the southern limits of Western Sahara. The Scotsman
Mackenzie signed a trading agreement in 1879 to establish his North-West
Africa Company with a trading post at Tarfaya, a little beyond Western
Sahara's northern edge. Spanish Sahara started with the colony of Rio de
Oro (later renamed Villa Cisneros and then Dakhla). Founded as a trading
post in 1884, it was attacked by a Saharan tribe, the Oulad Delim, and its
stores looted before a royal decree placed the entire coast from Cape Boujdour to Cape Blanc under Spanish administration, as confirmed by the Congress of Berlin, General Act. Two years later, Spanish colonial jurisdiction
was extended 150 miles inland, and after another two years of fighting with
Sahrawis, an agreement was reached with a shaikh of the Oulad Delim.

In 1900 France and Spain signed a convention delimiting their respective possessions in the Saharan coastal region. The frontiers of Spanish
Sahara followed the imperial pattern. A boundary line was to divide the
Cape Blanc peninsula, splitting it in two equal parts, natural features permitting, before continuing north, then east at 21°20' latitude north to the
intersection of this parallel by the meridian 15°20' west of Paris (13° west
of Greenwich). From that point the line of demarcation would extend northwest, creating a curve between the 15°20' and 16°20' meridians west of
Paris (13° and 14° west of Greenwich). Where the curve met the meridian
15°20' west of Paris, the frontier would stretch as directly as possible to the
intersection of the Tropic of Cancer and the meridian 14°20' west of Paris
(12° west of Greenwich) and continue northward on that meridian.[2] The
Morocco Agreement, signed in Paris in 1904, completed the northern frontier with a demarcation line between the French and Spanish "spheres of influence" to start from the intersection of the meridian 14°20' west of Paris
with latitude 26 north and to follow it east until meeting the meridian 11
west of Paris, then along that meridian as far as the Draa Wadi. The curve
in the southwestern corner carved out a chunk of territory for the benefit
of France. It effectively assigned to French interests the salt mines of the
Idjil region. These were of the greatest importance to the caravan trade,
which traveled on routes from the Niger and Senegal through present-day
Mauritania and across the Sahara, from Adrar to Tindouf and on to the Draa
Wadi. Later the same area was to acquire new value with the profitable
extraction of iron ore deposits and their transshipment by train for export
from the port at Nouadhibou, in Mauritania.

The European powers continued bickering over the region. The most
powerful, Great Britain and France, saw Spanish interests reduced but still
important. By the 1930s, Spain controlled a number of territories in northwest Africa. These varied considerably in size, history, and status. The
ancient enclaves of Mellila and Ceuta had been under Spanish rule since,

respectively, 1497 and 1580; also in northern Morocco was Spain's protectorate over the Rif. To the south, again within the kingdom of Morocco, were Ifni and Spanish Southern Morocco, and beyond that Villa Cisneros, as Rio de Oro was now called, and La Guera at the Mauritanian border. In 1946, after World War II, a decree created the Spanish West Africa administration to comprise Ifni, Tarfaya and Spanish Southern Morocco, and the Seguia el-Hamra and the Rio de Oro. El-Ayoun (Laayoune), which had been founded in 1940 when an ample supply of fresh water was verified, became the administrative center of Spanish West Africa and was confirmed by decree as provincial capital in 1958. After Morocco's independence from French protectorate in 1956 had forced Spain to recognize Moroccan sovereignty, the Spanish dictator General Francisco Franco relinquished Tarfaya and Spanish Southern Morocco in 1958. In the same year Spanish West Africa was officially abolished by a decree that converted Spanish Sahara and Ifni into provinces of Spain, Ifni having been ceded to Spain "in perpetuity" under a treaty in 1860.

For the kingdom of Morocco, the French withdrawal was a dramatic but only partial victory. The Spanish enclaves remained in the north, and Spain controlled other parts of Moroccan territory. But how much was truly "Moroccan"? The leader of Morocco's independence party, Istiqlal, declared: "So long as Tangier is not liberated from its international statute, so long as the Spanish deserts of the south, the Sahara from Tindouf to Atar and the Algerian-Moroccan borderlands are not liberated from their trusteeship, our independence will remain incomplete and our first duty will be to carry on action to liberate the country and to unify it."[3] This was the idea of "Greater Morocco." The most ambitious claims, however, were gradually discounted. Morocco refused initially to countenance Mauritania as an independent state by opposing its admission to the UN, then relented, and following a brief war with Algeria it renounced any title to Tindouf. But Morocco never wavered in asserting its right to recovering the Spanish possessions or the king in his mission to "unify" the nation.

Spanish Sahara and Ifni were considered by the UN (Decolonization) Committee of 24 in 1964: at that time the population of Ifni was estimated at 50,000 and Spanish Sahara at 24,000. In December 1965, the UN General Assembly decided that both Ifni and the Saharans had the right to freedom from "colonial domination" and called on Spain to "enter into negotiations on the problems relating to sovereignty presented by these two Territories."[4] Spain and Portugal voted against this resolution, and France, South Africa, the United Kingdom, and the United States abstained. Morocco, while not believing that its claim to Ifni and Spanish Sahara required confirmation, seemed comfortable with assuming the population's wish to "return to the motherland." Outbreaks of fighting linked to Morocco's Army of Liberation and attacks on French interests in Mauritanian iron ore had precipitated the militarily successful Ouragan operation conducted jointly by French and Spanish forces, but Madrid eventually recognized its relative weakness and in 1969 ceded Ifni to Morocco. Spanish Sahara was another matter. Having earlier been a purely prestige asset, the territory now showed signs of bringing profit. The discovery of high-grade phosphate rock at Bou Craa led to heavy investment in mining equipment and the construction of a conveyor belt—at 62 miles, reputedly the world's longest—and new port facilities at Laayoune. Spanish interests in off-shore fishing were undiminished. Spanish Sahara also provided continental backing for the Canary Islands.

Moroccan stability was rocked in 1971 by a coup attempt against King Hassan II as he celebrated his forty-second birthday. Hassan survived, only to be subjected to a second attack on his life the following year, when disloyal air force officers sought to shoot down the aircraft in which he was flying back from France. The king emerged unscathed and determined. Generals were harshly reduced in number by various means, and a new constitution was promulgated. In 1973, King Hassan himself took command of the Royal Armed Forces (FAR); he "Moroccanized" foreign-owned farms and enacted other political measures edging gradually toward liberalization and parliamentary elections. In 1974 he proclaimed a "holy war" to recover "Moroccan Sahara," in an appeal to patriotism and to consolidate royal prestige. For the officer corps this was to become a cause, while keeping the army at an appropriate distance. King Hassan saw his place in history as the "reunifier" of the nation, following in the footsteps of his father, who had achieved independence from France.

An unpretentious resistance movement to Spanish rule in the Sahara emerged in 1972. MOREHOB (Mouvement de Resistance "Les Hommes Bleus") was founded in the Moroccan capital, Rabat, only to peter out within a year. In 1973, the Frente Polisario came into being, its leadership drawn principally from Sahrawis who had been studying or living in Morocco, and it evolved rapidly as a force to be reckoned with. Disturbances in the territory and mounting political pressure, externally and internally, drove Spain to propose a declaration of internal autonomy as a step toward full self-determination. It was decided that a population census would be carried out. At the same time, the Spanish authorities worked to foster a political climate favorable to themselves. They authorized a political party, at first announced to be "revolutionary" and "progressive," but it was committed to modernization in keeping with conservative values and to preserving special relations with Spain. In February 1975 it was registered, more appropriately as the Partido de la Union Nacional Saharaui, the PUNS.

In 1975, activity escalated in every sphere. The UN Committee of 24 dispatched a mission of inquiry in May—Spain had previously refused permission—and the day before the mission was to arrive, troops mutinied.

The mission, led by the Ivorian ambassador to the UN and including colleagues from Cuba and Iran, was greeted by mass demonstrations in Laayoune before traveling widely across the region.[5] The Spanish authorities seemed surprised by the enthusiasm for the Frente Polisario and the lack of evident support for their preferred PUNS. Within the week, the PUNS leader, Khalihenna Ould Rachid, had left for Morocco and declared allegiance to the king. As acts of violence continued, including serious sabotage to the phosphate conveyor belt, UN Secretary-General Kurt Waldheim made an effort to defuse the conflict: he visited the region from 9 to 13 June to urge a four-way conference, but without success.[6]

King Hassan endeavored to persuade Spain to make a joint appeal to the International Court of Justice (ICJ) for a nonbinding advisory opinion, presumably in the expectation that the principle of territorial integrity would prevail, thus avoiding recourse to a referendum that could lead to confrontation and conflict. When Spain proved unwilling, Hassan went to the World Court, with Mauritania, via the UN. The court, having given due consideration to the submissions received, announced its conclusions on 16 October 1975:

> The materials and information presented to the Court show the existence, at the time of Spanish colonization, of legal ties of allegiance between the Sultan of Morocco and some of the tribes living in the territory of Western Sahara. They equally show the existence of rights, including some rights relating to the land, which constituted legal ties between the Mauritanian entity, as understood by the Court, and the territory of Western Sahara. On the other hand, the Court's conclusion is that the materials and information presented to it do not establish any tie of territorial sovereignty between the territory of Western Sahara and the Kingdom of Morocco or the Mauritanian entity. Thus the Court has not found legal ties of such a nature as might affect the application of resolution 1514(XV) in the decolonization of Western Sahara and, in particular, of the principle of self-determination through the free and genuine expression of the will of the peoples of the Territory.[7]

The "legal ties of allegiance" to some tribes and indications of some display of the sultan's authority sufficed for King Hassan to interpret the ICJ ruling in Morocco's favor. He announced the launch of the "Green March," green being the holy color of Islam, which would allow thousands of Moroccans to march across the border and expel the "colonialist infidels from Moroccan soil." The formidable logistics required for moving 350,000 people were already well in hand. The king touched a popular nerve, and volunteers, many more than expected, had to be selected by quota and lottery. The great multitude gathered at Tarfaya just north of the border to await their king, Commander of the Faithful, as leader.

For Spain it was the worst possible timing. Generalissimo Franco, having but recently recovered from serious phlebitis, presided over the Spanish cabinet when it decided to turn to the UN Security Council, while at the same time it planned to transfer power to Polisario. Franco, now eighty-two years old, was taken sick again and in the days following suffered a series of heart attacks; he lay in a coma. The Spanish military was resolutely opposed to caving in to Morocco and had the means to resist. The 61,000-strong FAR faced 20,000 Spanish troops in Western Sahara with overwhelming reserves available in the Canaries and beyond, including the Spanish air force. However, 18,000 Spaniards living in Morocco, Ceuta, and Melilla posed a problem. Spain asked the king to postpone the march. The king claimed this to be impossible but revised the date to 28 October. A deal was then reached for Spain to open a 10-kilometer demilitarized zone inside the northern frontier, which would permit the marchers to enter before withdrawing. Further postponement of the march fixed the date for 4–6 November.

The United States and France, the two most interested powers outside the region, perceived King Hassan as an important ally, anticommunist, sympathetic to the North Atlantic Treaty Organization (NATO), helpful in dealings with Israel, and ruler of a country strategically situated at the entrance to the Mediterranean. U.S. secretary of state Henry Kissinger was reported to have said that he would "not allow another Angola on the east flank of the Atlantic Ocean."[8] Kissinger was in Rabat in late 1974, and in October 1975 Alfred Atherton, an assistant secretary of state, visited Morocco again while General Vernon Walters, trusted presidential emissary, went to Madrid. Spain was still urging the Security Council to insist, not merely request, that King Hassan desist from the march, but the king rejected further conciliatory efforts as overtaken by events and gave the order on 5 November. The following morning the marchers in their thousands crossed into Spanish Sahara brandishing the Quran and waving Moroccan flags before dropping to the ground, facing Mecca, to pray and give thanks to the Almighty. Many who took part still recall the experience with emotion.

On 8 November 1975, the government of Spain agreed to hand over the Sahara to Morocco and Mauritania without conducting a referendum. As Franco lay dying, the Madrid accords, concluded on 14 November, formally ceded the territory, and Spain committed itself to withdraw by the end of February 1976.[9] The views of the Saharan population, as expressed through the Djemaa Council of chiefs and representatives (more correctly the Asamblea general del Sahara), would be respected.[10] Other details remained secret but were believed to have included concessions to Spain concerning phosphate and mineral extraction as well as coastal fisheries. By the end of November, Hassan declared the Saharan dossier closed.

* * *

But for Algeria it was not closed. Algeria had found the Security Council lily-livered; not surprisingly, its urgent "request" rather than "order" to end the march had been ignored. President Houari Boumedienne threatened Hassan: "I am not like Christ. I will not offer my cheek for a second blow. I shall respond to the utmost of my ability."[11] As Moroccan armed forces moved in to establish control, large numbers of Sahrawis left the towns and settlements. The Red Cross reported 40,000 refugees fleeing eastward. At Amgala, a staging post some 180 kilometers from the Algerian border, Algerian soldiers were sent "to assist." Moroccan forces attacked, killing some and capturing ninety-nine. Boumedienne withdrew the Algerian troops. Three weeks later when Polisario was reported to have "massacred" Moroccan soldiers at Amgala, Hassan blamed Algeria. Morocco was alleged to have deployed air power, even napalm, to attack refugee concentrations at Guelta Zemmour and Oum Dreyga. Before the end of the year, the UN High Commissioner for Refugees (UNHCR) gave an estimate of 50,000 Saharan refugees in southern Algeria.[12]

When the Djemaa was convoked in special session on 29 November, only 32 of its 102 members arrived; 67 members were said to have been meeting with the Polisario at Guelta Zemmour the previous day, when they voted to dissolve their assembly. The UN was also divided. The General Assembly adopted two resolutions that December. One, without referring to the Madrid Accords, requested Spain as the administering power to take all necessary measures so that the people of Spanish Sahara might exercise fully and freely their inalienable right to self-determination.[13] The other took note of the Madrid tripartite agreement and endorsed steps to ensure respect for the freely expressed aspirations of "all the Saharan populations originating in the Territory," who "would be able to exercise their inalienable right to self-determination through free consultations organized with the assistance of a representative of the United Nations appointed by the Secretary-General."[14] Waldheim dispatched the Swedish ambassador, Olof Rydbeck, who after visiting the area from 7 to 12 February reported that genuine consultation was not possible.[15] Just before the deadline for Spanish withdrawal, the Djemaa met on 26 February. There was no UN presence, and Spain refused to recognize the session as constituting the "popular consultation" envisioned in the Madrid agreement. This time 57 of the 102 members attended, and they voted unanimously to approve the decolonization of the territory and its "reintegration" with Morocco and Mauritania.

Spanish civilians had been evacuated, corpses of Spaniards had been exhumed and shipped out, and even animals from the zoo had been taken away when, on 26 February 1976, two days early, Spain took its final leave of what had been Spanish Sahara and delivered the territory to Morocco and Mauritania. A day later, at Bir Lahlou, the Provisional Sahrawi National Council declared Western Sahara an independent state and raised its flag: it was to be known as the Sahrawi Arab Democratic Republic, SADR in English though better known by its French acronym RASD. Leaders of the Frente Polisario were appointed to key offices. The next day Madagascar recognized the SADR, to be followed by Burundi. When, on 6 March 1976, Algeria officially recognized the new state, Morocco broke off diplomatic relations with Algiers.

Notes

1. For the geographical background and summarized history of Western Sahara, see John Damis, *Conflict in Northwest Africa: The Western Sahara Dispute* (Stanford, Calif.: Hoover Institution Press, 1983); Tony Hodges, *Western Sahara: The Roots of a Desert War* (Westport, Conn.: Lawrence Hill, 1983); John Mercer, *Spanish Sahara* (London: George Allen and Unwin, 1976); Robert Rezette, *The Western Sahara and the Frontiers of Morocco* (Paris: Nouvelles Editions Latines, 1975).

2. Rezette, *The Western Sahara*, 64–65.

3. Quoted in Bertrand Fessard de Foucault, "La question du Sahara espagnol," *Revue Française d'Etudes Politiques Africaines,* year 10, no. 119 (November 1975): 78, and cited by Hodges, *Western Sahara,* 85.

4. UN General Assembly Resolution 2072 (XX), 16 December 1965.

5. Report of UN Visiting Mission to Spanish Sahara, May-June 1975, General Assembly Official Records, 30th session, suppl. 23, UN Doc A/10023 Rev 1.

6. Report of the Secretary-General in pursuance of Security Council Resolution 377 (1975), UN Doc S/11863 (31 October 1975).

7. International Court of Justice Advisory Opinion, 16 October 1975, conclusion.

8. Henry Kissinger "declared in Madrid that 'the United States will not allow another Angola on the East flank of the Atlantic Ocean'": Leo Kamil. *Fueling the Fire: U.S. Policy and the Western Sahara Conflict* (Trenton, N.J.: Red Sea, 1987), 10. No source given.

9. Although the Madrid Accords of 14 November 1975 were secret, the declaration of principles as made public indicated that Spain would withdraw from Spanish Western Sahara by the end of February 1976 and cede the territory to Morocco and Mauritania; it would proceed forthwith to institute a temporary administration in which Morocco and Mauritania would participate in collaboration with the Djemaa. See Hodges, *Western Sahara,* 223.

10. UN Doc S/11880 (19 November 1975), Annex III (Security Council Official Records, suppl. for October/November/December), 41.

11. Quoted in Anthony Pazzanita and Tony Hodges, *Historical Dictionary of Western Sahara* (Metuchen, N.J.: Scarecrow, 1994), 83; see also Adekeye Adebajo, "Selling Out the Sahara: The Tragic Tale of the UN Referendum," Cornell University, Institute for African Development, Occasional Papers Series, Spring 2002, 8.

12. UNHCR Program of Humanitarian Assistance in the Tindouf Area, Doc HCR/155/42/76.

13. UN General Assembly Resolution 3458A (10 December 1976).

14. UN General Assembly Resolution 3458B (10 December 1976).

15. Rydbeck's report was not published; it may have been thought too sensitive.

3

Conflict, the OAU, and the UN

Four events in short order had precipitated fundamental change in Western Sahara. The ICJ opinion was followed by the Green March, the Madrid Accords with Spain ceding power to Morocco and Mauritania, and the declaration of the SADR as an independent state. The rupture of diplomatic relations between Rabat and Algiers further heightened tension in the region. Rivalry between Morocco and Algeria was nothing new. Border disputes had led to fighting in 1963, and continuing animosity was fueled by their antagonistic systems of government and opposing geopolitical alliances. The common experience of the French, albeit on different terms, and the fact that they were roughly equal in population seemed to stimulate competitiveness.

After the clashes at Amgala, with troops killed and prisoners taken, war looked imminent until Algerian forces were withdrawn and Hassan decided not to act on a threat of hot pursuit. Diplomatic confrontation persisted. While Morocco took military and other measures to reinforce the defense of its "historic and legitimate" claim, Algeria campaigned to muster OAU and nonaligned backing for Sahrawi self-determination and the prospect of independence. In what was to become an enduring theme, Algeria insisted that this was not a bilateral dispute with Morocco, while Morocco argued that only Algerian material and political support made Polisario's existence possible—the refugee camps were all on Algerian territory—and the so-called SADR was not a legitimate state with which Morocco could negotiate.

After a lapse of time, in late 1977, the king ventured a tentative approach to Algeria by sending his sister, Princess Aicha, to Lausanne, Switzerland, to meet President Boumedienne's political adviser, Ahmed Taleb Ibrahimi. Ibrahimi had a further meeting with the king's adviser, Reda Guedira, in early 1978, but a projected encounter between the two heads of state, planned for Brussels later in the year, did not take place. As it was, Boumedienne fell

31

seriously ill and died that December. His successor, Chadli Bendjedid, was expected to be more amenable.

* * *

Meanwhile the situation on the ground shifted. The Frente Polisario, from combating Spanish colonialism, turned its attention to Morocco and Maurita- nia. Although heavily outnumbered by the FAR, the Polisario forces had the advantage of familiarity with the terrain and were well armed, well organ- ized, and highly motivated. When they concentrated their attacks on Mauri- tania, the consequences were eventually decisive. The Mauritanian leadership was ousted in a military coup, and when Mauritania failed to honor an agree- ment to withdraw from territory that it continued to occupy, the Polisario broke the cease-fire. Negotiations followed, and on 5 August 1979 a peace agreement was signed in Algiers, ending Mauritania's involvement in West- ern Sahara. An originally secret provision would have handed over the south- ern part of the territory to Polisario upon Mauritanian withdrawal, but neither the Polisario nor Morocco welcomed a Saharan ministate. Moroccan forces moved in promptly to occupy the area vacated by Mauritania. The Polisario, having dealt effectively with Mauritanian interests, focused its firepower on Morocco with considerable success. It achieved some notable military incur- sions, even deep into Moroccan territory, to the great embarrassment of Rabat, but could not defeat the Moroccan armed forces.

Fighting in Mauritania and the abrupt change of government jolted the OAU into action. At the Khartoum summit in July 1978, an ad hoc com- mittee of at least five heads of state was set up to address the problem; it was to be known as the Committee of Wise Men.[1] The Wise Men made lit- tle progress, partly because Morocco refused to recognize Polisario as a negotiating partner and Algeria refused to negotiate on behalf of Polisario. The following year, at the Monrovia summit, the OAU adopted a resolution calling for a cease-fire and the holding of a free and fair referendum in which the Sahrawi people could exercise their right to self-determination with a choice between total independence and preservation of the status quo. Twelve months later, there was movement to admit the SADR as a member state of the organization. Toward the end of the same year, the UN General Assembly called on Morocco to begin negotiations with Polisario.

Arguably in an effort to forestall the SADR's recognition as an OAU member state, and probably responding to the counsel of friendly powers, King Hassan chose the OAU summit at Nairobi in 1981 to declare that he would accept a "controlled referendum whose modalities would give justice simultaneously to the objectives of the *ad hoc* Committee, that is to say the Committee of Wise Men, and to Morocco's conviction regarding the legitimacy of its rights."[2] On returning home, he interpreted the referendum as an act of confirmation and named the interested parties as Morocco, Algeria, and Mauritania. According to Moroccan foreign minister M'Hammed Boucetta, "Polisario is not recognized as a liberation movement. What is called the SADR is not recognized as a state," and the king could negotiate only with recognized states.[3]

Algeria resented Morocco's refusal to deal with the Polisario and began lobbying to have SADR admitted to OAU membership. When at the presummit meeting in 1982 the Frontline States of southern Africa pressed for SADR's election, Morocco and eighteen other members of the organization walked out. The summit, which was to be held in Libya, did not take place. The nineteenth OAU summit in June of the following year adopted a resolution naming Morocco and the Polisario Front as "parties to the conflict" and calling for direct negotiations leading to a referendum of self-determination.[4]

Meanwhile, King Fahd of Saudi Arabia succeeded in having King Hassan and President Chadli Bendjedid meet in their first face-to-face encounter in four years. This was the occasion when Hassan reportedly hinted, "Leave me the stamp and the flag [the symbols of sovereignty]; all else is negotiable."[5] Unfortunately, the outcome of the meeting failed to match the optimistic mood. Bendjedid, in his supposed willingness to accommodate Morocco, may have been overruled by his own military hard-liners; it is more than plausible that high-level Algerian opinion was split. The most positive result seems to have been that Algeria was willing to use its influence with Polisario not to press for OAU membership and that Morocco, in return, would agree to some direct contact. Three of Hassan's most senior counselors and ministers met secretly with three Polisario leaders three months later, in April 1983.

If 1983 had been characterized by modest movement toward compromise, 1984 turned to a hardening of positions. In August, Morocco astounded observers with a crafty move: an alliance with Libya. The Treaty of Oujda between the two countries prevented Libya from continuing to arm the Polisario. Then in September, King Hassan addressed the UN General Assembly; saying: "Morocco tells you that it wishes a referendum. Morocco tells you that it is prepared to hold this referendum as of tomorrow if you want. Morocco is ready to grant all the conditions necessary for all observers wherever they may come from so that there can be a cease-fire and so that a just, fair and true consultation may follow. Finally, Morocco is solemnly committed to the results of the referendum."[6] In November at the OAU summit, after some procedural maneuvering, the SADR became a full member of the organization, and Morocco left, depriving the OAU of an important founding state and one of the parties to the dispute. The UN General Assembly called again for direct negotiations.[7]

The next April, in Lisbon, Morocco's minister of interior, Driss Basri, met Polisario's number two, Mustapha Bachir Sayed (brother of El-Ouali, the front's founder, who had been killed while fighting in Mauritania). But there was no substantive dividend. A month later, King Hassan rejected as not serious an Algerian proposal that he preside as king of Morocco and also as king of Western Sahara. In the autumn, the Non-Aligned Movement urged direct negotiations, and in December the UN General Assembly, reflecting an OAU decision, called for direct negotiations, a cease-fire, and a referendum.[8]

The UN became seriously implicated in 1986. Secretary-General Javier Perez de Cuellar offered his good offices with a view to arranging indirect talks between the parties. These took place in New York in April and again in May. The chairman of the OAU was represented, and Algeria and Mauritania were kept informed; this was to become the pattern. Morocco and Polisario were each given a questionnaire to which they responded, but when Perez de Cuellar visited the region in July, he encountered little progress. Although Morocco refused to accept direct talks as a condition for UN mediation, it agreed to the notion of UN supervision of a referendum. Polisario argued for a UN-supervised referendum, direct UN administration of the territory, a joint UN-OAU security force, and withdrawal of Moroccan forces and settlers from the territory before the vote.[9]

Morocco had the advantage of U.S. sympathy and practical support under the Ronald Reagan administration. Among other things, the king was helpful to the United States on Middle Eastern matters. As chairman of the El Qods Committee of the Arab League, he met in Rabat with Israeli prime minister Shimon Peres. This meeting led to Libya's terminating the alliance of two years earlier; its purpose had, however, already been achieved. Equally significant, a great defensive wall encircling Western Sahara was nearing completion: it ran from the Moroccan border with Algeria in the north around the "useful triangle" of Laayoune, Bou Craa, and Smara, skirted the eastern frontier with Mauritania (at sufficient distance to permit hot pursuit), and stretched to the southern limits of the territory near the sea, some 2,000 kilometers in all. The wall, known as the berm, was constructed of sand and stone with manned and fortified posts at regular intervals across its entire length; it was equipped with listening devices and protected by minefields. Although it could be breached, it rendered more difficult the raid-and-return incursions that Polisario had carried out earlier with some impunity. It enabled Morocco to establish its military superiority.

In an effort at further negotiation, King Fahd of Saudi Arabia mediated a second encounter between King Hassan and President Bendjedid, this time at Akid Lotfi on the Algerian-Moroccan border. Saudi Arabia had leverage—it was believed to contribute $1 billion a year to Morocco—and King Fahd, who was personally present, was expected to exercise a conciliatory influence. Although the meeting was not as productive as had been hoped, there were results. An exchange of prisoners of war followed, improved relations opened the way for a UN fact-finding tour of the region in late 1987, and a year later diplomatic relations were reestablished between Algeria and Morocco.

One of the conditions for the renewal of diplomatic ties, it was believed, was a political solution in Western Sahara,[10] which had to be read between the lines of a joint Algerian-Moroccan communiqué:

> Eager to promote the success of international efforts undertaken to hasten the process of good offices for a just and definitive solution to the Western Sahara conflict through a free and regular fair referendum for self-determination held without any constraints whatsoever and with utmost sincerity . . . [Algeria and Morocco] have decided to reestablish diplomatic relations.[11]

The news was welcomed abroad. Improved relations between Algeria and Morocco could be only beneficial to the wider region and to prospects for cooperation and development in the Maghreb. There were those who expected the Sahrawi cause to suffer in consequence. This seemed almost inevitable if the Western Sahara issue were to be resolved in such a way as not to disrupt good relations between Morocco and Algeria. The king, when interviewed in early August, talked of the Sahrawis' being granted autonomy if they decided to remain Moroccan; he was totally opposed to independence.[12]

* * *

In July 1998, the Saudis again tried to be helpful, this time at a less exalted level. They organized secret talks at Ta'ef in Saudi Arabia. Little beyond the fact of meeting was achieved.[13] Then, on 11 August 1988, following earlier separate meetings in Geneva, the UN Secretary-General and a special envoy of the then chairman of the OAU presented Morocco and the Frente Polisario, again separately, with a document, framed as a joint UN-OAU plan for a UN-supervised cease-fire and referendum, with "proposals for a just and definitive solution of the question of Western Sahara in conformity with General Assembly resolution 1514 (XV) . . . to enable the people of Western Sahara, in the exercise of their right to self-determination, to choose between independence and integration with Morocco."[14] No third alternative was envisaged. On 30 August, both sides informed the Secretary-General of their "agreement in principle" while "making comments and observations."[15] The Secretary-General provided the Security Council with an outline of the settlement proposals, informing the Council at the same time of the parties' agreement in principle, but without spelling out their observations. On 20 September the Security Council approved.[16]

That October, the Decolonization Committee of the UN General Assembly, the Fourth Committee, took up the Western Sahara issue and adopted a draft resolution calling for direct negotiations. The resolution was passed in plenary on 22 November with a General Assembly recorded vote favoring negotiations by 86 votes to none with 53 abstentions.[17] Morocco saw the call for direct negotiations as being at variance with the Secretary-General's initiative. Nevertheless, the king agreed to a meeting with the Sahrawis that would include representatives of the Frente Polisario.[18] The king insisted, according to the press, that he would meet the Polisario for "discussion," not "negotiation." They met on 4–5 January 1989 in Marrakech. The Sahrawi delegation—Bachir Mustapha Sayed (the Frente Polisario's number two), Mahfoud Ali Beiba, and Brahim Ghali—carried a signed-and-sealed SADR mandate to negotiate as plenipotentiaries. They were received by the king, alone. His most senior cabinet members remained outside the audience chamber. From what Polisario said afterward, King Hassan told the Sahrawis: "Despite all the investments I have made in the territory, I haven't succeeded in winning your hearts. There has been too much bloodshed, we need to put an end to this conflict."[19] He did not wish to leave a "time-bomb" for his son, the crown prince. There was no agreement on autonomy, Polisario stated. What was expected was that they would meet again.

In the Moroccan view, Polisario abused the meeting to imply a degree of political recognition. The king maintained that he had received "Moroccans who have gone astray . . . in the hope that they would be put back on the right path. Never were they received as members of the so-called Polisario."[20] He reaffirmed that Western Sahara was Moroccan territory: Morocco, he declared shortly after the meeting, "will not give an inch of its territory."[21] King Hassan then repeated his promise to the Sahrawi nationalists that "when they have reintegrated their homeland, they would benefit from the regionalisation plan which has been envisaged."[22]

Further talks did not materialize. In March 1989, the Frente Polisario ended the unilateral cease-fire that it had declared a month earlier. This coincided with the inauguration, after years of rhetoric, of the Arab Maghreb Union (AMU) as a union of Algeria, Libya, Mauritania, Morocco, and Tunisia—without the SADR. A new round of talks was promised for September, but it was aborted. The king maintained that it was superfluous: "There is nothing to negotiate because Western Sahara is Moroccan territory."[23] Renewed military operations by Polisario were also given as a reason.[24] Polisario, frustrated at the lack of progress, attacked positions along the sand wall, or berm, in October and November.

Notes

1. The presidents chosen at the Khartoum summit, 18–22 July 1978, were those of Sudan, Tanzania, Mali, Nigeria, Ivory Coast, and Guinea (UN Doc. A/33/337, 31 October 1978).

2. King Hassan, quoted in *Le Monde,* 28–29 June 1981; cited by Tony Hodges, *Western Sahara: The Roots of a Desert War* (Westport, Conn.: Lawrence Hill, 1983), 311.

3. Boucetta as quoted in *Le Matin,* 10 February 1982; cited by Hodges, *Western Sahara,* 314.

4. Agence France Presse dispatch from Addis Ababa, 11 June 1983; cited by Hodges, *Western Sahara,* 316.

5. The phrase was regularly repeated whenever the early stages of the conflict were under discussion. It is quoted by Paul Balta, *Le Grand Maghreb: Des indépendances à l'an 2000* (Paris: La Decouverté, 1990), 181, 228.

6. A. Berramdane, *Le Sahara Occidental* (Paris: Enjeu Maghrebin, 1992), 93, as translated in Yahia H. Zoubir, "Protracted Conflict and Failure to Achieve Prenegotiation in the Western Sahara Conflict," *Humboldt Journal of Social Relations* 20, no. 2 (1994): 17.

7. UN General Assembly Resolution 39/40 (5 December 1984), operative par. 3.

8. UN General Assembly Resolution 40/50 (2 December 1985).

9. *New York Times,* 1 July 1985, referred to by William J. Durch, "Building on Sand: UN Peacekeeping in the Western Sahara," *International Security* 17, no. 4 (Spring 1993): 157.

10. *Africa News,* 30 May 1988, and *Guardian,* 28 September 1988, cited by Yahia H. Zoubir, "Origins and Development of the Conflict in Western Sahara," in *International Dimensions of the Western Sahara Conflict,* ed. Yahia H. Zoubir and Daniel Volman (Westport, Conn.: Greenwood, 1993), 8.

11. *El Moudjahid,* 17 May 1988, and *New York Times,* 17 May 1988, cited by Zoubir, "Origins and Development," 8.

12. *Le Monde,* 3 August 1988, cited by Yahia H. Zoubir, "Protracted Conflict and Failure to Achieve Prenegotiation," in *International Dimensions of the Western Sahara Conflict,* ed. Yahia H. Zoubir and Daniel Volman (Westport, CT: Greenwood, 1993), 22–23.

13. Zoubir quotes a Polisario official as saying, "A member of the [Moroccan] royal family did come; he said: 'You are meeting, that's good!' Then he left" ("Protracted Conflict," 23).

14. Report of the Secretary-General, S/21360 (18 June 1990), par. 1.

15. Ibid., par. 2.

16. Security Council Resolution 621 (1988), 20 September 1988.

17. UN General Assembly Resolution 43/33 (22 November 1988).

18. *Le Point,* 12 December 1988, and *New York Times,* 28 December 1988, cited by Zoubir, "Protracted Conflict," 25; see also *Le Monde,* 25–26 December 1988 and 27 December 1988.

19. See Zoubir, "Protracted Conflict," 27.

20. Agence France Presse, 16 January 1989, cited by Zoubir, "Protracted Conflict," 28.

21. Ibid.

22. *Le Nouvel Observateur,* 12–18 January 1989, cited by Zoubir, "Protracted Conflict," 28.

23. *West Africa,* 2–8 October 1989, cited by Zoubir, "Protracted Conflict," 29.

24. *El Sharq al Awsat,* 10 October 1989, cited by Zoubir, "Protracted Conflict," 29.

4

Toward Settling the Conflict

UN Secretary-General Javier Perez de Cuellar played a critical role and kept his cards close to his chest. In elaborating both the original proposition—the proposals and implementation plan for the settlement of the Western Sahara dispute first put to the Security Council in 1990[1]—and the more detailed implementation plan submitted in 1991,[2] he delegated broad responsibility to a trusted member of his immediate staff, Issa Diallo, special assistant and a director in the executive office. The Task Force for Western Sahara, the high-level committee composed principally of under-secretaries general, was not consistently involved, nor always fully informed, a fact that was much resented by at least one member[3] and that served to compound misunderstanding. Diallo conducted negotiations with the Moroccan representatives and with Polisario separately and in the strictest confidence. The reservations both sides expressed when conveying their agreement in principle, besides not being passed to the Security Council, were not even revealed to the task force. When the text of what was proposed came before the Council two years later, both Morocco and the Frente Polisario reacted vehemently; it was as if they had not agreed to the same plan.

The plan presented to the Council in June 1990 included provision for a cease-fire, phased troop withdrawal and confinement, repatriation of refugees, transitional arrangements leading to a referendum, a supervisory role for the special representative—who was to have sole and exclusive authority over every aspect of the referendum—and an outline timetable.[4] A seemingly straightforward section at the heart of the Secretary-General's submission dealt with the manner of determining those eligible to vote in the referendum. It was treated as a technical exercise. An Identification Commission composed of expert personnel—"a population expert familiar with the problems and features of Saharan society, assisted by three to five specialists in the demographics of countries whose population is predominantly

39

nomadic"[5]—would review the 1974 census (conducted by the Spanish administration shortly before its departure) and update it. That entailed calculating the real growth of the Saharan population in the period between the census and the referendum, taking into account births (although in 1990 or 1991, anyone born after 1974 would not yet have reached the qualifying age of eighteen) and deaths as well as movements of the Saharan population. After completing its preliminary research, the commission was to meet in the presence of tribal chiefs, who would be asked to comment and contribute. Representatives of the two parties and of the OAU would also be invited to attend as observers. The implementation plan, based essentially on the settlement proposals and attempting "to meet, to the greatest extent possible, the major concerns of the parties," deemed eighteen weeks from the coming into force of the cease-fire as sufficient for the purpose.[6] The identification procedure looked almost innocuous beside the more obviously contentious issues pertaining to the reduction of forces, the confinement of troops, security, and the maintenance of law and order in the territory. The Security Council approved the Secretary-General's report containing "the full text of the settlement proposals as accepted by the two parties"[7] and called on the parties to cooperate fully.

Morocco countered with a fiercely critical twelve-page letter to the Secretary-General. In this letter, dated 30 July 1990, King Hassan made clear the limits to his earlier acceptance in principle of the original proposals and showed his frustration with the plan submitted to the Council as failing to take into account Morocco's expressed concerns and serious reservations. The letter was not communicated to Council members, nor was it shown to the responsible group in the UN Secretariat, the Task Force for Western Sahara.[8] In October Morocco decided to issue the letter as a press release. The communication dealt at length with administrative responsibility, the maintenance of law and order, security issues, and the armed forces, but it also noted that the eighteen weeks envisaged for the Identification Commission to complete its work was insufficient, "exaggeratedly optimistic taking into account the complexity of the operation" and "the difficulties which may arise in establishing an electoral roll." Another paragraph spelled out the "problem of taking into account in establishing the electoral lists of Saharans who sought refuge in Morocco when the Territory was under Spanish domination."[9]

The Frente Polisario also responded promptly, on 4 August, with its comments. These too remained confidential until, some time after the Moroccan press release, they were issued publicly on 26 November by the Polisario office in New York.[10] The Frente Polisario wanted to emphasize a role for the UN in administering the territory, with access to Western Sahara during the transitional period "in order to avoid [an influx] of foreign population."[11] The communication then highlighted the identification of those who would be entitled to participate in the referendum and insisted:

> The elaboration of the settlement plan of the Western Sahara conflict gained momentum only when the Sahrawi people took the responsibility to make the sacrifice in accepting the Spanish census of 1974 as the only and unique basis for the preparation of the electoral lists. This compromise was accepted by the two parties and provided for in the conclusions approved by the Security Council.
>
> This is a fundamental principle whose respect is a condition for the success of the authenticity of the referendum, particularly because of the limited number of the population concerned by the referendum. . . .
>
> Thus the intransigence must guide the preparation of the electoral lists, in conformity with the inviolable agreement contained in the United Nations' plan. It is also true that the up-dating of the 1974 census cannot have any other meaning than the spelling correction of names or the deletion of the names of deceased persons.[12]

It was all too evident that both Morocco and the Frente Polisario recognized the basis for establishing the electoral roll as a determining issue, one where compromise could prove elusive, if not impossible. The fault line was manifest, but the Secretary-General and the Security Council chose to overlook arguments undermining that indispensable "agreement in principle." They may have hoped for a miracle: it has been suggested that Diallo was able to convince Perez de Cuellar that international pressure would prevail upon the parties to comply with the plan as proposed, that it would be "all right on the night."[13] I doubt it. A much more plausible explanation is the Secretary-General's assuming that encouraging signals from the region—the restoration of diplomatic ties and meetings between King Hassan and President Chadli Bendje40did and also with the Polisario at Marrakech—gave legitimate cause for optimism and that a negotiated deal might be in the offing, to form the basis for an act of self-determination. In such an event, the plan could be used to endorse whatever had been resolved at the highest level.

Perez de Cuellar certainly craved some result from the considerable effort and personal involvement he had invested. Time was running out: his term of office was due to expire at the end of 1991, and after nearly ten years labor on his exhausting "pilgrimage for peace"—the title he chose for his memoirs—he had no intention of seeking, or even accepting, a further term. There are hints that he may have had "an undeclared agenda with the Moroccans" and "was hoping that, before the end of his mandate, he could mediate a political deal based on enhanced autonomy for Western Sahara within the Kingdom of Morocco; approval of this would be the proposition on which the Sahrawis would vote in an eventual referendum."[14] In his

memoirs he actually says, "I was never convinced that independence promised the best future for the inhabitants of the Western Sahara."[15] Given the
known inadequacies of the settlement plan, Perez de Cuellar's intention
makes sense, though Emhamed Khadad, who was later to become the Polisario coordinator with MINURSO, seemed genuinely shocked when he
encountered this in writing. During an informal conversation in the refugee
camps near Tindouf, he asked whether I had seen the book, then just published. Perez de Cuellar, he said, had sounded a very different note in conversation with the Polisario when he emphasized the bond between Spanish
speakers.

A critical year for the UN preceded the Secretary-General's completing
the settlement plan with a second report to the Council.[16] "Close observers
suggest that the Secretary-General pushed MINURSO into the mainstream
of UN politics just then," in mid-April 1991 after the Gulf War, "in hopes
that some of the postwar euphoria would rub off on it."[17] With a timetable
and detailed plan of action, Perez de Cuellar elaborated in an important section on the identification and registration of voters. The first task of the
Identification Commission was to "implement the proposals, agreed upon
by the two parties, that all Western Saharans to whom the 1974 census
undertaken by the Spanish authorities related and who are 18 years or over
will have the right to vote, whether they are currently present in the Territory or living outside it as refugees or for other reasons."[18] The commission's mandate to update the 1974 census included removing the names of
those who had died and "considering the applications from persons who
claim the right to participate in the referendum on the grounds that they are
Western Saharans and were omitted from the 1974 census." Given the more
complex tasks being attributed to the Identification Commission, the Secretary-General intended to appoint its members, not, as earlier proposed, for
work during the transitional period but as soon as the Council decided to
establish the mission and before the cease-fire came into effect. It could
even begin work in the two-week period preceding approval of the budget.

After the first item on the timetable in the Secretary-General's report,
which was the appointment of the Identification Commission to proceed
"immediately to establish its rules of procedure, to update the 1974 census
and to arrange for appeals,"[19] a detailed calendar followed. It allowed six-
teen weeks before the start of the transitional period, with military deci-
siveness entitled "D-Day," when the cease-fire would come into effect. At
that point the commission would begin the identification—envisaged,
though not explicitly stated, as personal identification—and registration of
voters as well as hearing appeals against noninclusion on the published list.
Eleven weeks after D-Day, the identification and registration of voters
would be completed and the final list of voters, as approved by the Secretary-General, published. Tribal chiefs (shaikhs) of Western Saharan tribes

were being asked to contribute to the commission's work, and the Secretary-General reported that a preliminary meeting of tribal chiefs had already taken place in Geneva in June 1990. In addition to the shaikhs' contribution, the parties—Morocco and the Frente Polisario—and representatives of the Organization of African Unity would participate in the commission's work as official observers. A sequence of further steps would culminate in the return of refugees from the Polisario camps near Tindouf in Algeria and the holding of a referendum. The mission would finish its business between twenty-four and twenty-six weeks after D-Day, and the last personnel would be withdrawn shortly thereafter. It was estimated that the referendum could take place about thirty-six weeks after the General Assembly approved the budget.

Perez de Cuellar admitted that the plan could not meet all the concerns of the two parties and that compromises had had to be sought,[20] while recognizing that, as a condition for success, the mission "must operate with the full cooperation of the two parties."[21] On 29 April 1991 the Security Council endorsed the Secretary-General's proposal: the Council approved the report, expressed its full support, called upon the two parties to cooperate fully in implementing the plan, and decided to establish a United Nations Mission for the Referendum in Western Sahara—MINURSO—to carry out the plan.[22] Neither Morocco nor the Frente Polisario chose to add publicly to their original "agreement in principle," nor to subtract from the reservations already expressed. Nothing was signed. On 17 May the General Assembly approved a budget.[23]

The timetable presented to the Council in 1991 revolved around the day on which a cease-fire would come into effect. Prior to the cease-fire the Identification Commission had work to do; an administrative unit and a logistics battalion were to be deployed, as were signals and medical units. Once the cease-fire came into effect on D-Day, the transitional period would begin, and combatants would be confined to UN-designated locations; prisoners of war would be exchanged, a general amnesty would be proclaimed, political prisoners and detainees would be released, and the consolidated voter lists would be published. A drawdown of Moroccan forces from 100,000 to 65,000 was to be completed within eleven weeks at the same time as voter registration and publication of the final voter list, when repatriation would also start. Twenty weeks after D-Day the referendum was to be held. Once the results had been announced, MINURSO would begin to withdraw and would be gone inside a four- to six-week period. There was no provision for enforcing the outcome of the referendum should the losing side refuse to comply.

If it is true that Perez de Cuellar hoped MINURSO would benefit from the atmosphere prevailing after the successful expulsion of Iraqi forces from Kuwait, he was disappointed. When on 24 May the Secretary-General proposed that the cease-fire enter into effect on 6 September, marking the launch of the transitional period, both parties first accepted, but it became clear that apparent agreement concealed radical differences.[24] After an informal cease-fire lasting over two years, serious fighting resumed in the territory, including aerial bombardment. Perez de Cuellar took the decision to divorce the cease-fire from other aspects of the plan and have it become effective on 6 September anyway, although King Hassan warned him in August that he would not permit the regular deployment of MINURSO until the issue of voter identification had been settled.[25] By putting D-Day on hold and untying the cease-fire from the start of the transitional period and other events that had been meticulously linked in the settlement calendar, the Secretary-General effectively removed a valuable incentive to compromise. That same August, Morocco submitted a list of 120,000 names of potential voters additional to those included in the 1974 census, and on 18 September an estimated 170,000 persons began moving into Western Sahara to "facilitate" their identification by the UN. The plan was in trouble, and it was inevitable, given the difficulties already encountered, that the timetable would need radical adjustment. The slow progress, according to the Secretary-General, was "largely due to the complexity of the identification process whose purpose is to establish the list of those who would vote in the referendum. . . . The parties," he reported to the Council, "have tended to interpret differently the relevant paragraphs of the plan," and despite points of convergence, a "satisfactory reconciliation of their positions has not yet been achieved." Moreover, the "indispensable climate of confidence" had not been helped by the "well-known" news that "a number of persons who are claimed to belong to Western Sahara have been moved into the Territory,"[26] which was interpreted by critics as a violation of the spirit if not the letter of the settlement plan.

Whether in response to Moroccan pressure (a minor scandal jeopardized Perez de Cuellar's impartiality when the press reported his postretirement appointment to a directorship of a Moroccan holding company, although he denied it[27]), or under influence from powers friendly to Morocco, or convinced by his advisers, on 19 December 1991, less than two weeks before he was due to retire, Perez de Cuellar chose to present to the Security Council another report containing crucial new elements. This happened to coincide with the critical final phase of his involvement in resolving the conflicts in Nicaragua and El Salvador. The Secretary-General's report, submitted in accordance with the Council's request to be kept regularly informed about implementation of the settlement plan, was offered as a valedictory by Perez de Cuellar: "This opportunity to share with the Council my assessment of the situation is all the more welcome as I near the end of my term of office as Secretary-General."[28]

He reported that following the outbreak of hostilities, he had decided that the cease-fire should come into effect as proposed on 6 September 1991, in spite of the fact that it would not be possible "to complete . . . a number of tasks that were supposed to be completed before the cease-fire." He conceded that "notwithstanding the parties' earlier acceptance of the plan, substantial areas of difference remained." One party—it was not declared which—was unable to agree that the transitional period begin on 6 September as envisaged. The inevitable adjustment to the timetable as originally proposed was attributed largely to "the complexity of the identification process, whose purpose is to establish the list of those who would vote in the referendum. The parties have tended to interpret differently the relevant paragraphs of the plan. . . . The cooperation of the parties was rightly identified . . . as an essential condition for its successful implementation." The Secretary-General reported progress in the deployment and activity of military observers and in logistics but referred again to "some parts of the identification process" as the exception, adding: "Without the active assistance of the Western Saharans themselves, and notably their leaders, the UN cannot carry out the complex identification task in a timely and effective manner." He insisted that the mandate of the Identification Commission and instructions for its work, annexed to the report, "constitute a just and fair basis for the conduct of the referendum."[29]

The tone remained technical. Wishful thinking assumed that much of the work could be handled by experts and the problems resolved through rational, informed argument. Outside observers, including many members of the Security Council, preferred it that way. Few, even in the region, began to understand the arcane nature of Sahrawi social organization and grasped the political implications, which precluded a purely technical approach. Morocco and the Frente Polisario knew otherwise. They realized that the conflict could never be cooperatively settled through procedures and a winner-take-all referendum fully acceptable to both. The Frente Polisario remained fervently committed to an electoral roll based exclusively on the Spanish census of 1974, inflated at most by a small margin of persons who had been missed, as conceded by the Spanish authorities. Morocco had no intention of submitting to a referendum with the stark choice between independence and integration on terms that nullified their broad definition of Sahrawi and consequently excluded many of those who might thus be qualified to vote. Details could be tinkered with, but compromise was impossible on the basics.

The Secretary-General concluded his valedictory report to the Council on a downbeat note. After mentioning differences of interpretation relating to the confinement of troops, the return of refugees and other Saharans living outside the territory, the number of persons claimed to belong to Western Sahara who had been moved into the territory, and the delay this engendered, he was obliged to accept, "with great regret," the resignation of his special representative, Johannes Manz.[30] Manz, a Swiss diplomat, was already the second person appointed as special representative; he had replaced Hector

Gross Espiell, a Uruguayan lawyer who went on to become his country's foreign minister. Manz left to be Switzerland's permanent observer at the UN; he may have wanted to resign because of that mass movement into the territory—the second Green March, as it was sometimes called—or he may have been encouraged to depart for less principled reasons, given his difficulty in working with other senior staff and the task force's dissatisfaction.[31] Whatever the reason, he already found it an impossible mission. Perez de Cuellar ended saying that he himself did "not wish to sound unduly optimistic. . . . Serious efforts will have to be made at the political and technical levels in order to keep the process going."[32]

More combustible matters were left to the detailed annex to the report of 19 December 1991, "Instructions Relating to the Tasks of the Identification Commission." The Secretary-General assumed—an assumption that Polisario of course found inflammatory—that the Spanish census of 1974 could not constitute the complete list of those qualified to participate in the referendum. This was the conclusion to be drawn from the Saharans' nomadic way of life, with ebb and flow across national borders, persons fleeing colonialism and conflict over many decades, individuals and families seeking refuge outside the territory for personal and economic reasons, for education and more. The Spanish authorities themselves had conceded that the census teams did not reach all Saharans in the territory. The tribal chiefs recognized that "many Saharans and Saharan refugees were omitted."[33] The Identification Commission was to use all available resources and expertise—particularly the tribal chiefs and notables, whose role could hardly be overemphasized—in identifying those qualified to vote.

A set of specific criteria offered justification for eligibility that went far beyond the Spanish census of 1974 and what the Frente Polisario had signaled as its acceptance limit. In addition to persons included in the census, Saharans present in Western Sahara at the time but not counted were admissible together with members of their immediate family—parents and children. Two other categories would open the door further to children of a Saharan born in the territory and to Saharans who had lived in the territory for six years consecutively or twelve years intermittently prior to 1975. Whereas those in the census and even some not counted had Spanish documentation to substantiate their identity, the last two groups did not. They depended on oral testimony, which was deemed admissible in keeping with Saharan tradition.[34]

* * *

How did the Security Council react? Most revealing is the account provided by the then U.S. assistant secretary of state for international organization affairs, John Bolton. Speaking later at the 1998 Congressional Defense and

Foreign Policy Forum, he summarized the situation as understood by the United States. It was obvious that "one of the critical questions was going to be the issue of who was eligible to vote." After checking testimony he had given in early 1992, he confirmed the United States to have estimated, since "no census is perfect and people could have been missed," that the "number of 74,000 might be increased by 10,000 names."[35] Operational programming and the budget had proceeded on that basis. Morocco's proposing 170,000 new names raised a major problem.

However, "because Secretary-General Perez de Cuellar had invested so much of his personal time and energy and, indeed, in his own mind at least, so much of his prestige trying to resolve the Western Sahara, we were content, for well or ill, to let him pursue his own negotiations." Bolton qualified that by continuing:

> At the same time we were looking at ways to resolve the situation in Nicaragua and El Salvador, in which we had also invested a considerable amount of time and effort, and which faced the same midnight, December 31st deadline. And as the Security Council and the various contact groups working on Central America on the one hand and the Western Sahara on the other, got to Christmas time in 1991, it became increasingly clear that we were going to resolve one of these issues or the other. Perez de Cuellar had twenty-four hours in six or seven days left, and we were prepared to take every single one of those hours, and pretty much did take every one of those hours. But, it was beyond any human ability to do more than one of these at the same time. . . .
>
> And certainly . . . it will come as no surprise that within the US government's deliberations on which priority we felt was higher, Central America won. And, in fact, we were able to sign in Mexico City in January of 1992, a series of agreements that brought the situation in Central America to resolution. But, that meant that we had failed in the Western Sahara. And, in fact, so badly did we fail, that when the Secretary-General brought in the last days of 1991, a new report to the Security Council which proposed new criteria by which voter eligibility could be established, we felt that his work was simply unacceptable; that the new criteria did not match our understanding of what the parties had previously agreed. Indeed, our understanding at the time was that the parties themselves, or at least one of the parties, were not going to agree to what the Secretary-General had come up with. That left us in a difficult position on Perez de Cuellar's last day of office: do we endorse a Security Council resolution that says, "We reject this report"? Sort of a stinging way for a Secretary-General to go out of office, especially at the same time he is hopefully delivering, along with our efforts, a solution in Central America.
>
> So . . . we agreed on a resolution in the Security Council that would—and I use the precise word—"welcome" the Secretary-General's report. It did not approve the report. It did not approve the voter criteria. It didn't disapprove it. It simply welcomed it. So, I suppose you could "welcome" a cold rain, too. I mean you could welcome a lot of things. That was the word we came up with, recognizing that we were imminently to have a new Secretary-General.[36]

The welcoming resolution was adopted on New Year's Eve.[37]

* * *

The newly elected Secretary-General of the UN, Boutros Boutros-Ghali, took advantage of the Heads of State and Government meeting of the Security Council in January 1992 to touch on Western Sahara in his informal contacts. U.S. president Bush was present, as was King Hassan of Morocco (Morocco had been elected to, and had just assumed, a two-year nonpermanent seat on the Council). Boutros-Ghali seems to have agreed with Perez de Cuellar that "Morocco would not accept a vote in favour of independence" and contemplated the idea of asking the Security Council to endorse renegotiation of the settlement proposals.[38] Meanwhile, he put the emphasis on having the parties confer. To apply pressure he suggested appointing an American as the new special representative; according to Bolton, he was perceived as wanting to have an American involved in order to "bring this thing to resolution."[39] The name of General Vernon Walters was talked of, but he was unable or unwilling to accept, and it is difficult to see how someone so close to the Moroccans could have been made acceptable to the Polisario. In March 1992, Sahabzada Yaqub-Khan was appointed. Yaqub-Khan was a patrician Pakistani, well seen in Washington, with an immensely distinguished career behind him: he had risen to lieutenant-general in the army, had been appointed governor of East Pakistan (now Bangladesh), and had served as Pakistan's ambassador in Paris, Washington, and Moscow before becoming foreign minister. He was also a gifted linguist. The one problem, from the Polisario point of view, was his closeness to King Hassan.

"Everything stopped at that point," according to Bolton. "Everything stopped."[40] Very far from the truth, but it is true that progress was painful, slow, and intermittent. The premise of willing cooperation by the parties, with neither pressure nor coercion in prospect, the divided sympathies of Security Council members, and the problems of identification—arcane and alien to all but initiates—rendered compromise all the more elusive. Morocco and the Polisario had not, in their hearts, agreed to the same settlement plan, and at each step of the way they resisted any move that threatened their particular interpretation.

Morocco was still reticent about the full deployment of MINURSO, pending acceptance of Perez de Cuellar's proposals for identification. There were delays to the transfer of vital supplies for the military observer component—communications equipment and air-conditioning units that were indispensable for desert team sites. The ruling that all shipments be unloaded at Agadir in Morocco, rather than at the port of Laayoune, capital of Western Sahara, where the mission was headquartered, added eight or more hours of arduous and costly cross-desert travel. These impediments were eventually surmounted, and the military observers were allowed to monitor the cease-fire. That worked. The cease-fire continued to hold despite, in the early period, a large number of reported nonviolent violations, mostly over-flights; and these gradually diminished. MINURSO benefited from the participation, for the first time in a peacekeeping mission, of contingents from all five permanent members of the UN Security Council. Russia had proposed this innovation, a change from the convention that Permanent Five nationals not serve in the military component of peacekeeping operations, and the United States, initially opposed, came to agree. The United Kingdom withdrew its contingent in late 1993 when the former Yugoslavia placed heavy demands on peacekeeping personnel, but the other four—China, France, Russia, and the United States—continued to provide military observers.

In other respects, progress was effectively deadlocked. The revised list of persons included in the 1974 census had yet to be published in the territory, although both sides claimed to have communicated it to the Western Saharans concerned. There was still no sign of agreement on the eligibility criteria. No instructions could therefore be issued on how to apply for inclusion. In February 1992, the Secretary-General informed the Council that without an understanding on the eligibility criteria and related aspects of the identification process, including the selection and role of tribal chiefs and observers, implementation of the settlement plan would "remain blocked." He concluded that if after three months at the end of May there was still no agreement, it would "be necessary to consider alternative courses of action and possibly adopt a new approach to the whole problem." The UN, he added, had "never before organized a referendum of this kind."[41] There was no precedent. Essential to any hope of success was the full cooperation of the two parties, which was not forthcoming.

No progress had been made by the end of May. To give Yaqub-Khan, who had been appointed on 23 March, more space in which to have the parties talk, the Secretary-General proposed that the Council authorize a three-month extension. He repeated: "If by that time the peace process remains deadlocked, notwithstanding the efforts currently being made by my Special Representative in his talks with the parties, the Security Council might wish to consider a different approach."[42]

As a means to an end, Yaqub-Khan tried adapting the subject matter, to make talks more "user friendly." Although "fully cognizant that disagreements over the criteria for eligibility to vote in the referendum are the main obstacles," discussion would be encouraged to focus on "the formulation of safeguards to protect the political, economic, social and other rights and liberties of the losing side in the referendum."[43] The intention was principally to bring the two sides together with a view to promoting an improved atmosphere, to stimulate a little more trust and confidence. This succeeded to the extent that both parties were reported as ready to engage in a further round of talks, talks that would this time be devoted to the main contentious issue: the interpretation of the criteria for eligibility to vote. Not that their respective positions had changed. Morocco accepted the criteria proposed on 19 December 1991, notwithstanding its reservations concerning certain provisions that it found inappropriately restrictive, in particular the restriction to one generation of Sahrawis' being allowed to vote in the referendum. The Polisario rejected the criteria as "a violation of the settlement plan"; though prepared to accept some elements, it maintained fundamental reservations regarding others—all those relating to persons not connected in any way to the 1974 census.[44]

Meanwhile, to the consternation of the Polisario, Morocco was reported to be planning to hold municipal and legislative elections and a plebiscite on constitutional reform in which the inhabitants of Western Sahara would vote. These were not the first elections organized by Morocco in Western Sahara, but they would be the first to occur in the presence of the UN. Morocco signaled its reluctance to accept any postponement, arguing that the elections had already been deferred from early 1990 and were "quite independent of and separate from the holding of a referendum under the UN plan."[45] Voting took place on 4 September 1992. The constitution, as amended, introduced the "region" as a new administrative subdivision, and on 8 September, King Hassan announced that Western Sahara would form the first such region and enjoy priority in terms of development. Municipal elections followed a month later.

There was no progress report in September, nor in November as the Secretary-General had intimated to the president of the Security Council, nor December. There was no progress to report. In January 1993 Boutros-Ghali explained that the delay was due to the difficulty of convening a meeting of tribal chiefs.[46]

The position of the parties was unchanged. Morocco continued to insist, "All persons having Saharan status should have the right to participate in the referendum and . . . accordingly, Saharans who for various reasons were omitted by the Spanish authorities in 1974 should be considered on the same basis as those who were counted; hence, Morocco regards the list of persons counted in 1974 as a point of reference for the establishment of the electorate."[47] The Frente Polisario remained adamant that "in the initial agreement, the two parties agreed that the 1974 list would be the sole basis of the electorate and that, accordingly, the Saharans counted in 1974 should constitute the vast majority of persons authorized to participate in the referendum, while Saharans omitted from the census should constitute an exception to that group."[48] It was intimated informally that a 10 percent increase might be acceptable, but no more.

Equally incompatible were their views on acceptable evidence. The Frente Polisario "emphasized the special importance of written evidence emanating from the Territory, in other words, authentic documents issued

by the Spanish authorities in Spanish Sahara"; Polisario distrusted documentation provided by Morocco and had little confidence in oral testimony,
which it thought unreliable and open to abuse.[49] Morocco insisted, with
similar conviction, on the "equal importance, in a nomadic and traditional
society, of oral testimonies and official documents, regardless of their
source."[50]

The gathering of tribal chiefs, when finally organized, did nothing to
help. Nineteen shaikhs designated by Morocco and nineteen by Polisario
were invited to Geneva. There was a dispute about the legitimacy of some
participants on the Moroccan side, and the consultative meeting had to be
canceled. (Unkind tongues recalled a hotelier's welcoming their departure
and insinuating that Sahrawi shaikhs on an earlier visit had satisfied their
craving for very strong home-brewed tea on Primus stoves in their rooms
and burned holes in the carpet!) This setback, according to the Secretary-
General, "demonstrates starkly the futility of the efforts undertaken with
vigor and resource . . . to seek a way out of the existing deadlock." He registered his frustration at being no closer to resolving the voter list impasse
than twelve months earlier and felt constrained to put to the Council a
choice between three broad options. One would be the continuation of talks,
and chances for success were "very slim"; the second to implement the plan
according to the criteria of 19 December 1991, "which may mean that the
implementation would have to proceed without the cooperation of one
party."[51] The third choice was to adopt an alternative approach, yet again.

The Secretary-General's report in January 1993 confronted the Council
with a dilemma.[52] The first option sounded hopeless, the second looked to
some members like capitulation to Morocco, and the third meant abandoning the settlement plan. The French representative, who had, incidentally,
been ambassador to Rabat, presented a draft resolution in favor of option
two. The Frente Polisario reacted strongly with a letter to the Council president insisting that a people with the right to self-determination would not
take part in an operation lacking credibility and reiterating that Perez de
Cuellar's criteria constituted a "flagrant violation" of the peace plan. The
draft resolution was withdrawn; the U.S. representative, under the new
Democratic administration of Bill Clinton, demanded the consent of both
parties to any proposed solution. A decision was postponed until 2 March,
when the Council, coincidentally with the Moroccan ambassador presiding,
opted to forge ahead with a powerful resolution in the hope that both sides
would cooperate in keeping the process alive.

Resolution 809, when adopted, led to a surge.[53] Gentle persuasion by
interested and sympathetic countries may have helped budge the parties
from their most entrenched positions. Or the shifts may have been tactical.
The Frente Polisario, while tenaciously clinging to the 1974 census and still
rejecting the validity of oral testimony, had a real interest in seeing the plan

proceed. Morocco was possibly waiting for the Polisario to challenge what
it considered deceitful maneuvering and abandon the process, which would
free the Council to endorse "proceeding without the cooperation of one
party." Meanwhile, Morocco was prepared to move ahead cautiously, provided always that the Perez de Cuellar criteria were applied and that oral
testimony was accepted as valid. By May 1993 the Secretary-General felt
justified in confirming that both sides showed "a desire to move towards an
early referendum." They had expressed a desire to proceed promptly with
the registration of voters and agreed to the participation of tribal chiefs as
well as observers from both sides in the registration process.[54]

In that light, it was decided to reestablish the Identification Commission. The newly appointed chairman had already arrived in the region; as an
assistant secretary-general, I became the senior MINURSO appointee in the
mission area, since Yaqub-Khan worked out of New York. Yaqub-Khan
readily bequeathed to me what he termed the "technical" aspects, leaving
himself to concentrate on achieving a politically negotiated solution through
talks, which was still deemed the most realistic option.

Following a June visit to northwest Africa, Boutros-Ghali announced at
a press conference in Geneva on 2 July that direct talks, under UN auspices,
would take place in Laayoune. The Polisario made known its agreement the
next day. Driss Basri, the Moroccan minister of interior, affirmed on 7 July
that Morocco welcomed the Polisario representatives "with open arms,"[55]
and in a broadcast speech on 8 July, King Hassan expressed the hope that
the meeting would be an occasion of "tolerance and reconciliation and that
we may be able to build together a united country."[56] The meeting, which
took place in Laayoune from 17 to 19 July, was characterized in an opening
message from Boutros-Ghali as "historic." Yaqub-Khan arrived from New
York to launch the proceedings; he stated that the declared purpose of the
meeting was to explore the best ways of implementing the settlement plan
and to examine perspectives for the future.

It had been assumed that the Moroccan side would be led by Ahmed
Snoussi, ambassador, permanent representative of Morocco to the UN, and
reputedly a good friend of the king, with Mohammed Azmi, a governor
from the Ministry of Interior who was expert in Saharan affairs, as a member of the delegation. Snoussi and Azmi were present, but the delegation
was announced as representing the Royal Consultative Council on Saharan
Affairs together with the Moroccan ambassador to the UN and a senior representative of the Ministry of Interior. The effective leader, it emerged, was
Mohammed Sheikh Biadillah, a Sahrawi who, like some of the other delegates, was drawn from the Royal Consultative Council. As broadcast on
Radio Algiers, the Polisario representative, Mohamed Lamine Ahmed,
denounced the so-called Consultative Council on Saharan Affairs as having

no legal status and as being used in an attempt to legitimize the occupation by one country of another. He insisted that Morocco had assured the Frente Polisario that the Moroccan delegation would have Snoussi as its head, and had then substituted a member of the so-called Consultative Council on Saharan Affairs.[57] That Biadillah had himself once been sympathetic to the Polisario cause and that his brother, to whom he bore an uncanny physical resemblance, sat opposite as a member of the Polisario delegation did nothing to reduce tension. Polisario's representatives had as leader Mustapha Bachir Sayed, the organization's charismatic number two, and six members of their political directorate.

The opening session took place at MINURSO headquarters, an appropriate setting for the Secretary-General's introductory message, and as Polisario preferred. The front sought symbolic neutrality under the flag of the United Nations—although its members expressed discomfort at the Moroccan flag's prominence near the entrance of the building. The Moroccans wanted the next session to be on their terrain, on an alternating principle, and proposed the conference room at the Hotel Parador, where most of the delegates from both sides were accommodated. As in all public rooms in Morocco and the territory it administered, this room featured a portrait of King Hassan. Polisario asked that the king's picture be removed for the course of the meeting; it could perhaps be taken down for cleaning. The Moroccan delegation refused: such a mark of disrespect, amounting to *lèse majesté,* was out of the question. After the opening session on 17 July, Yaqub-Khan was unable to obtain agreement to a further meeting. Morocco was unwilling to return to MINURSO premises, and the Polisario would not contemplate sitting under the king's watchful gaze. An uncomfortable day's negotiation failed to bridge the differences, and after heated exchanges between Yaqub-Khan and Bachir, the Polisario decided to return home. Only a telephonic intervention from the United States persuaded them to stay another night.

The following day, 19 July, an ingenious compromise was achieved when both sides accepted an encounter, without a formalized meeting, in the grand hotel salon, where a small fountain and decorative rivulet divided the space in two; the king's picture could be interpreted to be on the other bank of the stream. Snoussi was able to act out his instructions to focus on ways and means of integrating the "Sahrawis of Tindouf" into Morocco in the context of regionalization as decided by the king; he delivered King Hassan's greeting to the Frente Polisario representatives with the words "You are our sons and you are in your country." When Bachir spoke, it was to say that they had come in order to facilitate implementation of the settlement plan. Although he felt that there was little to show for the meeting, he considered it valuable as a step toward dialogue. When the Polisario delegation departed for the airport—they were flown to and from Tindouf in UN air-craft—one of their number trailed miniature SADR flags from the car, a prank that provoked fierce consternation in the Moroccan camp.

Although nothing substantive had been achieved, the Secretary-General in his next report quoted the president of the Security Council as calling Laayoune a "positive development."[58] At a meeting of its national secretariat from 11 to 13 September, the Frente Polisario decided that it wished to continue dialogue and direct negotiation with Morocco. Algeria's foreign minister, Mohamed Salah Dembri, declared that it was more impor-tant than ever that dialogue resume between Morocco and the Frente Polis-ario at a responsible level.[59]

Yaqub-Khan planned a further round of talks that October, in New York during the General Assembly session, which meant exposure to polit-ical fireworks. The talks failed to materialize. The Frente Polisario rejected a Moroccan delegation composed exclusively of members of the Royal Consultative Council on Saharan Affairs and including two former leading Polisario personalities who had transferred their allegiance to Morocco: Brahim Hakim and Omar Hadrami. In Bachir's words, "This is not a Moroccan delegation; this is a delegation of *'transfuges'* and Sahrawi deserters. They represent nothing at all."[60] A spokesman for Morocco dis-missed "direct" negotiations with the Frente Polisario, claiming that the purpose of the meeting was to permit Sahrawis to discuss between them-selves prospects for the future of the territory in the context of the Moroc-can community—an attitude that the U.S. ambassador to the UN, Made-leine Albright, qualified as "provocative."[61] That Morocco sent to New York a delegation of Sahrawis, including eminent defectors, offended the Polisario, and Morocco was offended by Polisario's attempts to exploit a degree of recognition. Both felt deceived, and the two delegations never met. When after three days it was still proving impossible to arrange a meeting, Boutros-Ghali was obliged to abandon, for the time being, any hope of organizing direct talks.[62]

That effort was, if anything, counterproductive. The failure, which both sides attributed partly to bad faith on the other's part, did nothing to rem-edy the lack of trust or reverse the loss of confidence. When Yaqub-Khan visited the region in early November, he was accused by Polisario of spend-ing a mere four hours in the Tindouf area and failing to see its leader, Mohamed Abdel-Aziz, while staying several days in Rabat, "where he par-ticipated in ceremonies commemorating the Green March"[63]—which was highly unlikely! In early January 1994, the special representative returned for more time with the Polisario and was snubbed with subtle elegance. He was received and escorted by Abdelkader Taleb Omar, the SADR "minis-ter of interior," an articulate and charming man who was not mandated to discuss issues relating to the referendum. After luncheon, Yaqub-Khan was entertained in one of the refugee camps by a folkloric show, with dancing, chant singing, and ululating that seemed to last forever. In the evening he waited until Abdel-Aziz, the Polisario secretary-general, arrived and dinner could be served in a schoolroom. There were no speeches. After eating, Abdel-Aziz said good-bye and left.

* * *

I had meanwhile been instructed by Boutros-Ghali, in absolute secrecy, to invite Abdel-Aziz to Geneva in January 1994. The Secretary-General also asked King Hassan to be represented. The king dispatched one of his closest and most senior advisers, General Khadiri, together with Snoussi, but Abdel-Aziz, despite urging by the Secretary-General, did not consider the level appropriate in relation to himself, and nothing came of the proposed encounter. Boutros-Ghali, who knew Khadiri as one of two key advisers to the king on Western Sahara and a privileged channel of communication, believes that Abdel-Aziz may have been alarmed by his suspicion that it was Khadiri who had induced Brahim Hakim to transfer his allegiance from Polisario to Morocco.[64]

The reality was that Frente Polisario wanted to talk, to negotiate—that was a priority—but the person of the interlocutor was crucial. Apart from questions of status, Polisario leaders believed that the concentration of political power in Morocco made it meaningful to talk only to King Hassan himself or to the crown prince; all others lacked the necessary authority. They especially resented being faced with the Sahrawis who had betrayed their cause or were directly associated with those they labeled traitors. Although Polisario leaders were convinced that their claim to independence would be well served by a referendum, provided that the voters' list was limited to persons covered by the 1974 census, they seemed equally certain that Morocco would resist that and that there was no international will to compel Morocco to comply. Thoroughly disenchanted by Perez de Cuellar's revised criteria as "welcomed" by the Security Council, they had little confidence that the settlement plan could be implemented in a manner acceptable to themselves.

Morocco's king remained personally and publicly committed to a "confirmatory" referendum: the reunification of his realm through the recovery of the areas once controlled by France and all the enclaves acquired by Spain, including the former Spanish Sahara. To that end he was prepared to talk, not negotiate, with those Sahrawis who were to be welcomed back into the fold. He had, after all, expressed a willingness to consider every aspect, except the flag and the stamp—always provided no "recognition" of the SADR was implied—hence the imperative for total discretion. Once the Sahrawis were ensconced within Moroccan sovereignty, details of relative autonomy could be discussed; the regionalization policy was already a beginning. Senior Moroccan officials said that they had been instructed to study models based on Spain's provinces and Germany's *länder*.[65]

There was no effective pressure, international or otherwise, to make concessions. The Moroccans wanted to see whether the revised criteria for identification and acceptance of oral testimony would render the plan an acceptable instrument to deliver the result they desired. They were in no hurry. Change on the ground was working in their favor.

Notes

1. Report of the Secretary-General, S/23160 (18 June 1990).
2. Report of the Secretary-General, S/22464 (19 April 1991).
3. Marrack Goulding, *Peacemonger* (London: John Murray, 2002), 204.
4. Report of the Secretary-General, S/21360 (18 June 1990).
5. Ibid., par. 26.
6. Ibid., par. 46.
7. Security Council Resolution 658 (1990), 27 June 1990.
8. Goulding, *Peacemonger,* 206.
9. MAP (Moroccan Press Agency) press release, referenced Maroc/Onu/Sahara, 19 October 1990; quotes from pars. 5, 6, 12.
10. Frente Polisario Office at the United Nations, New York, press release of 26 November 1990.
11. Ibid., sec. I, par. 2.
12. Ibid., sec. II, pars. 1–2.
13. Goulding, *Peacemonger,* 202.
14. Ibid., 211–212.
15. Javier Perez de Cuellar, *Pilgrimage for Peace* (New York: St. Martin's, 1997), 352.
16. Report of the Secretary-General, S/22464 (19 April 1991).
17. William J. Durch, "Building on Sand: UN Peacekeeping in the Western Sahara," *International Security* 17, no. 4 (Spring 1993): 159.
18. Report of the Secretary-General, S/22464 (19 April 1991), par. 20.
19. Ibid., par. 52.
20. Ibid., par. 54.
21. Ibid., par. 55.
22. Security Council Resolution 690 (1991), 29 April 1991.
23. UN General Assembly Resolution 45/266 (17 May 1991).
24. Report of the Secretary-General, S/23299 (19 December 1991), par. 3.
25. William J. Durch, "United Nations Mission for the Referendum in Western Sahara," in *The Evolution of UN Peacekeeping* (New York: St. Martin's, 1993), 428.
26. Report of the Secretary-General, S/23299 (19 December 1991), pars. 8, 11.
27. "After he retired, Perez de Cuellar was reportedly appointed to the board of a Moroccan-owned holding firm, Omnium Nord Africa, and the international press accused him of malfeasance" (Jaret Chopra, "A Chance for Peace in Western Sahara," *Survival* 39, no. 3 [Autumn 1997]: 54). See further Teresa K. Smith de Cherif, "Western Sahara: A Moroccan-Style Election?" *Review of African Political Economy,* no. 58 (November 1993): 102.

28. Report of the Secretary-General, S/23299 (19 December 1991), par. 1.

29. Ibid., pars. 3, 8–10.

30. Ibid., par. 12.

31. Goulding, *Peacemonger,* 209–213.

32. Report of the Secretary-General, S/23299 (19 December 1991), par. 15.

33. Ibid., Annex, par. 15.

34. Ibid., Annex, secs. VII–VIII.

35. John Bolton, "Resolving the Western Sahara Conflict," transcript of the Congressional Defense and Foreign Policy Forum, Washington, D.C., 1998, 2–3.

36. Ibid., 3–4.

37. Security Council Resolution 725 (1991), 31 December 1991.

38. Goulding, *Peacemonger,* 212–213.

39. Bolton, "Resolving the Western Sahara Conflict," 4.

40. Ibid., 5.

41. Report of the Secretary-General, S/23662 (28 February 1992), pars. 25, 30, 32.

42. Report of the Secretary-General, S/24040 (29 May 1992), par. 11.

43. Report of the Secretary-General, S/24464 (20 August 1992), par. 6.

44. Ibid., par. 9.

45. Ibid., par. 11.

46. Report of the Secretary-General, S/25170 (26 January 1993), par. 1.

47. Ibid., par. 15.

48. Ibid.

49. Ibid., par. 17.

50. Ibid.

51. Ibid., pars. 31–32.

52. Ibid.

53. Security Council Resolution 809 (1993), 2 March 1993.

54. Report of the Secretary-General, S/25818 (21 May 1993), pars. 3, 5.

55. See Martine de Froberville, *Sahara Occidental: La confiance perdue* (Paris: L'Harmattan, 1996), 201.

56. As reported by Reuters, Rabat, 9 July 1993, from the speech of King Hassan II on the occasion of his sixty-fourth birthday. Cited in ibid., 201.

57. See ibid., 203n8.

58. Report of the Secretary-General, S/26797 (24 November 1993), par. 16.

59. See Froberville, *Sahara Occidental,* 313, entry for 5 October 1993.

60. See ibid., 205.

61. As reported in *Liberation,* 28 October 1993, cited in ibid., 206, and mentioned by Yahia H. Zoubir, "Protracted Conflict and Failure to Achieve Prenegotiation in the Western Sahara Conflict," *Humboldt Journal of Social Relations* 20, no. 2 (1994), 36.

62. Report of the Secretary-General, S/26797 (24 November 1993), par. 16.

63. Froberville, *Sahara Occidental,* 219. No source given.

64. Interview with Boutros Boutros-Ghali in Paris, 8 April 2003.

65. In confidential discussion.

5

Identification: Who Has the Right to Vote?

As chairman of the Identification Commission, I found it an advantage to be permanently in the mission area. I had constant interaction with the key personalities on both sides, whom I genuinely liked, and although these meetings were less frequent, I had regular opportunities for discussion with the responsible leaders in Algiers (Algeria) and Nouakchott (Mauritania). This made it possible to develop personal relations, even build a measure of trust in the wider climate of almost total mistrust. My first task, still characterized as "technical," was to launch the identification process. Although not made explicit, it was my impression, subsequently reinforced by word and in action, that I was not expected to succeed; meaningful action lay elsewhere. In reality, even voter registration, which sounded "technical" in New York, was the political hard core, as Morocco and Polisario knew only too well. It was why they fought so fiercely for their particular interpretation at every step toward formation of the electoral roll.

The Polisario position was straightforward and repeated to me at every one of our early discussions. It never budged from its focus on an electorate based on the 1974 census, revised to eliminate those who had died in the intervening years and to include the modest number of additional persons who had been inadvertently omitted at the time; Colonel Emilio Cuevas, the Spanish official responsible for the census, conceded that there had been oversights.[1] Polisario argued that the population of Western Sahara, whatever the tribal affiliations beyond the territory and earlier tribal history, had acquired a national identity before Spain left. It was for that people, and it alone, to exercise the right of self-determination.

Morocco's argument was more complex. It emphasized the historical roots, the traditional ties of allegiance which in that society were tantamount to common "nationality," and above all a view of the Saharan tribes as belonging to a much wider region than the territory, which was only an artificial colonial construct, just another Spanish enclave on Moroccan soil.

The fact that many Sahrawis, including several of the Polisario leaders, had been outside Western Sahara at the time of the census, mainly in Morocco, reinforced the argument: these were people who moved readily in and out of the territory to be with fellow tribesmen, to escape foreign domination, for education, commerce, and other reasons, and had been especially prone to do so during the years of Spanish colonialism.[2] Many had even fought with the Moroccan Army of Liberation. A decision on the fate of the territory, therefore, could be taken only by Saharans with links to Western Sahara.

The Polisario view translated crisply into action. Revising the census lists by dropping the dead and incorporating a few more names, before checking the personal identity of candidates, could have been completed in the time span originally envisaged. Accommodating the Moroccan position was another matter. The formula proposed in Perez de Cuellar's eleventh-hour criteria and admission of oral testimony infuriated the Polisario not merely for endorsing as valid the Moroccan argument but because they did not believe it could be convincingly implemented. Early efforts to achieve informed understanding leading to compromise were hampered by the obscure terminology used to describe Sahrawi society as much as the intractable positions of the two sides. Even the eyes of Arabic speakers glazed over when faced with many-page lists of barely pronounceable tribal groups and their subgroups: fractions, subfractions, and *ahel*.

The reality underlying the 1974 census categories took time to decipher largely because the clarifications provided by one side did not tally with what the other said. Neither disputed that the Spanish census had recognized the seven most important tribes of Western Sahara (the Reguibat Charg, Reguibat Sahel, Izarguien, Ait Lahsen, Arosien, Oulad Delim, and Oulad Tidrarin), but they differed about the other three "tribes" (Tribes of the North, Chorfa, and Tribes of the Coast and South). In truth these were tribal groupings—each of them encompassing a number of tribes—and had been so classified by Spain in order to accommodate persons living in the territory who were not members of any of the seven main tribes. They included individuals from a range of different tribes, some quite small, some very large, with the majority of their members living outside Western Sahara. To a noninitiate, tribes and tribal groupings looked much the same, with similar nomenclature and presented with a similar structure, but the implications were far-reaching.

From the Polisario angle, maintaining those three groupings, especially the eighth, the northern tribes, would throw the door wide open to an influx of vast numbers of pro-Moroccan voters, Saharans perhaps but with connections to the territory that were tenuous at best, simply because one or two of their number happened to be included in the 1974 census, and with their own shaikh to vouch for their Western Saharan antecedents. Polisario found it difficult to believe that the criteria would, even could, be rigidly applied. Hence their insistence on written proof in the form of Spanish documents, that is, documents issued before 1975. Oral testimony might easily be manipulated; what was more, after some twenty years the tribal leaders, the shaikhs, could hardly be expected to know all their people as in the past. Many shaikhs had died; they were already elders of the community when elected in 1973. Polisario was adamant that shaikhs appointed by Morocco since the 1973 election could not be trusted. As one explained to me: "They can all be bought. No shaikh is entirely trustworthy." "What about your own?" I asked. "Even them," came the reply, "but we have not the means. Morocco, though, has plenty of money."[3]

Each Sahrawi tribe was divided into "fractions," "subfractions," and family groups called *ahel*. For most organizational purposes and for social reference the key unit was the subfraction: individuals would identify themselves as belonging to a certain tribe and subfraction. Subfraction membership was similarly reflected in the census. Every subfraction of the known tribes—there were eighty-eight of these—had its tribal leader or shaikh, or more than one in cases of the large subfractions. The Spanish colonial administration had also attributed shaikhs to the tribal groupings. When the last election of shaikhs took place in 1973, the candidates were already mature men of standing in their community; twenty years later, when the UN came to draw up a definitive list of recognized shaikhs, one-third of those elected in 1973 were no longer living. Curiously, and it was one of the few surprises to make life less complex, the number of deceased and surviving shaikhs was equally divided between the Moroccan and the Polisario sides.

Several of the tribes had people living both in and outside the territory. About that there was no dispute. The annex to Perez de Cuellar's report of 19 December 1991 stipulated that "only members of a tribe whose connection with the Territory within the limits of recognized international borders is clearly established should participate in the referendum."[4] Further, "it is membership of a family group (subfraction of a tribe) existing in the Territory, which can be attested to by the sheiks [*sic*] and notables of the family group, that should eventually prevail for eligibility."[5] The category "subfraction" is here applied, but earlier in the same text "family group" had been defined as *ahel*.[6] The distinction was not unimportant, since some larger subfractions had many members living both within and outside the territory.

Morocco argued that the members of all subfractions of any Saharan tribe included in the census should be eligible for consideration, including those of subfractions not specifically listed. The Polisario insisted that unless the "great majority" of members of any subfraction had been counted in the 1974 census, that subfraction could not be considered as "existing in the territory" and its members, other than those named in the census, should not be eligible. They thought *ahel* the more appropriate unit of reference, but this was too social scientific for the outside world, which had problems enough with "fractions" and "subfractions." Nor was there any convincing way to calculate the "great majority" that Polisario wanted. The Secretary-General's compromise, to which they reluctantly agreed, was to admit the candidature of any person belonging to a tribal subfraction included in the census, regardless of the number counted. Members of tribes included in the census, but belonging to a subfraction not specifically listed, would not be accepted. This was a formula that might be made to work for the seven principal tribes; Moroccan experts and the Polisario knew that the three contested tribal groupings would not be susceptible to similar treatment.

In adopting Resolution 809 in March 1993,[7] the Security Council voted for a mandate favoring the second option to proceed in accordance with the 19 December criteria and requested the Secretary-General to prepare for the referendum by "commencing voter registration on a prompt basis starting with the updated lists of the 1974 census."[8] Whatever the real expectations, that was the task officially entrusted to me; it was to be carried out with "the full cooperation of both parties."[9]

The Frente Polisario adhered rigidly to the precise wording of the resolution. Polisario was comfortable with the updated lists of the 1974 census. Morocco, on the other hand, referring to earlier resolutions of the Council, rejected any distinction between those included in the 1974 census and other applicants. More important still, Rabat objected to any step toward identification, and that included preliminary registration, until the Perez de Cuellar criteria had been openly accepted by the Polisario.

The first thing was to publish the revised census lists, and with the parties' assistance it finally happened. The figure came to 72,370 names (out of the original Spanish census figure of 73,497 Saharans in a total population of 95,019). Procedures then had to be developed for application by potential voters and for the identification process itself. There was no precedent; as the Secretary-General said, the UN had not previously undertaken an exercise of this kind.[10] With the draft of a pioneer registration form, I visited Rabat, where the Western Saharan issue was handled by Morocco's strong man, the redoubtable minister of interior Driss Basri, answering to the king himself, and the Polisario camps at Rabouni, where Mustapha Bachir Sayed, the movement's impressive number two, was my principal interlocutor. Even a draft registration form posed problems. It had been assumed in New York that the language could be French in order to facilitate processing by mission staff (the UN's official working languages are English and French). This was at once rejected by Polisario, who suggested Spanish. Both sides also wanted Arabic. However, the names on the revised list appeared in the romanized alphabet. It was the immigration form used at airports in certain Arabic-speaking countries that suggested to me a registration *formulaire* in two versions: one with French reading from left to right and Arabic from right to left for each question, the other with Spanish and Arabic similarly patterned. Only the personal names had to appear in both romanized and Arabic script.

The questions to be answered were more contentious. The Polisario refused whatever went beyond the 1974 census, and Morocco rejected any wording that appeared to give "undue high relief" to persons included in the census as opposed to other applicants. According to Morocco, the UN should ask only about tribal membership. Polisario naturally wanted details of fraction and subfraction but also considered *ahel* to be "necessary, logical, and useful," as Bachir wrote in a letter to me.[11] Morocco was adamantly opposed. I made it clear to the Moroccans that "fraction" and, especially, "subfraction" were essential, since these were the defining terms used in Perez de Cuellar's annex; it was inconceivable that such information be omitted. That they came to accept, but *ahel* was out of the question. Polisario refused to surrender *ahel.* The compromise, which, I suspect, satisfied neither in almost equal measure, was to have one joint question about membership in a "subfraction/*ahel*," which I defended on the grounds that the Secretary-General's report referred to family group as *ahel* in one context and "subfraction" in another. Registration forms were printed accordingly in two versions, French-Arabic and Spanish-Arabic.

Polisario negotiators were still insisting that half the questions, those relevant to persons not included in the census, should not be on the form, and if they did appear they should not be numbered consecutively; applicants in the camps would not be completing that part, nor was it necessary. They stressed that, in conformity with Resolution 809, I was to begin with persons included in the 1974 census and had no business processing others. Morocco continued to reject any distinction between applications from persons in the census and from those who considered themselves qualified for other reasons. Morocco also continued to be firmly opposed to any move toward identification until Perez de Cuellar's criteria had been incontrovertibly accepted by Polisario. By the time Polisario was ready to start completing forms in the camps, it was also demanding that the process be launched simultaneously on both sides. Morocco showed no lessening of resolve until I suggested that we embark on registration, which would take some time, even if the processing of applications had to await agreement on interpretation of the criteria. For actual identification, I envisaged interviewing all potential voters by tribal unit in the presence of their respective shaikhs. As explained to the Council: "It would be more economical in time and effort, and more in accordance with the provisions of the settlement plan, to identify all potential voters from a given tribal unit simultaneously, rather than repeating the exercise in successive phases. . . . A simultaneous approach would be logistically more efficient and less likely to cause irregularities and confusions such as double entries."[12]

Bitterness and mistrust lingered on both sides: if there was no progress by the end of the year Polisario "could put matters in the hands of the military," as was said to me. Relations were not helped by the failed meeting in New York, but on 3 November 1993, as chairman of the Identification Commission, I was able to announce that registration would start, simultaneously, in the camps and in Laayoune. Ample supplies of the forms were made available; Morocco, having received 75,000, asked for an additional 125,000. Then another last-minute hitch occurred when the Moroccan minister of interior could not commit himself to a precise date without the king's authority. The king approved, though on the strict condition that no applications be processed until the criteria had been agreed. Basri relayed the royal verdict, adding that until such time as the criteria were agreed by Polisario, no completed forms would be returned to MINURSO from the Moroccan-administered areas. Once the criteria had been accepted, the forms would be submitted in bulk; I said that it was for individuals to apply, but this was dismissed as a technicality. Should the criteria not be agreed to by "the others," Morocco would destroy all such forms as had been completed.

The revised list (with a supplement listing those expected to reach the age of eighteen by year's end) was publicized on both sides in ten different places, and registration centers opened in Laayoune and the Tindouf area in late November. Few applicants were literate, and they depended on officials assigned to assist them as scribes. Some of the questions to be answered by persons not in the census were complex and involved the recollection of dates by people from a culture that was not date conscious. The form required time to complete. Both parties took this in hand, but as in other respects, what passed in the camps, where nearly all were included in the census, differed from the operation in Moroccan-administered areas, where the majority needed to respond to a series of questions in order to justify their claim. There were insufficient centers in Western Sahara to handle the many applicants, but the opening of additional centers became conditional on agreement on the wording of a joint public announcement. The communiqué was finally issued to the press on 8 February 1994. It announced the launch officially, provided relevant details, and confirmed 31 December 1993 as the date by which individuals had to have reached eighteen years of age to qualify.

Registration proceeded at centers in Laayoune and elsewhere. Members of the Identification Commission visited from time to time. There was more control by the parties than had been wished. The fact that the applicants were nearly all illiterate played into the hands of the scribe, which mattered most for persons not included in the census. One advantage was that Morocco and Polisario both seemed singularly well informed as to what was happening on the other side and took pains to warn me of any anomalies. When the time came for registration in Mauritania, where many Sahrawis were known to be living but the government insisted on maintaining a certain distance from the process so as not to prejudice its neutrality, MINURSO was enabled to muster the resources. MINURSO never had the means, nor was it expected, to handle the entire registration process in Western Sahara and the camps near Tindouf without the parties' cooperation.

Additional registration centers were opened, but Morocco remained adamant about needing to be absolutely certain that Polisario had accepted the criteria before agreeing to move beyond registration. Polisario wanted more assurance on the identification procedure, including the shaikh issue. But it was a start. Polisario was pleased to see the process under way at last. They gave the chairman a warm welcome in Rabouni to mark what they interpreted as a sea change in MINURSO. It was, however, only a start. The Polisario still wanted talks, with conditions. After Boutros-Ghali's unsuccessful effort to have Abdel-Aziz meet General Khadiri in Geneva, the Secretary-General was reluctant to try again too soon.

Pending acceptance of the 19 December criteria, we worked to develop an identification procedure that both sides could be persuaded to accept. In the terms of the plan, it was understood that Morocco and the Polisario would both be represented throughout identification, that the OAU would "observe" and tribal leaders assist. Although observation was not defined as necessarily constant, Polisario and the OAU demanded an uninterrupted presence. The procedure eventually agreed to was scrupulous and transparent. Once the completed registration forms had been received and their contents computerized, the commission would call forward applicants from a specific tribal group, an appropriate number each day at any given identification center. On arrival at the center, documents, if any, would be scrutinized, photographs and fingerprints taken, and the applicant's details and personal identity formally confirmed by one or both of the shaikhs present.

My proposal, indeed the only proposal that both parties would have accepted, was to have two shaikhs participate, one, and not more than one, drawn from each side, but both recognized tribal leaders of their particular subfraction. They were to be our expert witnesses. The shaikh would be called upon to confirm the personal identity of the applicant. Polisario was especially nervous that "the other side" would seek to present people under a false name, the name, for example, of someone listed who had died or was prevented from coming forward. In the event, this was one of the few problems not to arise. The shaikh would also be asked to vouch for the applicant's membership in the subfraction. Shaikhs of the old school had comprehensive knowledge of members of their subfraction and in most cases a phenomenal memory for names and relationships. Nearly twenty years' separation from those on the other side was a limitation, but because applicants had to be eighteen years or over, this affected fewer individuals, and the shaikh knew the family history for most of the candidates. The concept was admirable. The shaikh who recognized the subject would confirm his or her identity with the name or, in cases where the individual was not personally known, details of the family. In instances where the shaikh had compelling reason to be certain that an applicant was definitely not the person he or she claimed to be or a member of that subfraction, he could register a rejection—a "no" vote. It was assumed that in doubtful cases a shaikh would abstain, leaving the other shaikh's decision to prevail. All shaikhs swore an oath on the Quran before each session, and there was official confidence that these lords of the desert, *grands seigneurs* of irreproachable integrity, spoke only the truth.

Since the shaikhs had been elected in 1973 and were elders at that time, it was hardly surprising that many had not survived the intervening years. The Moroccans emphasized that the 1973 election had been for a five-year term, and they submitted a long list of notables who had been named shaikh subsequently in addition to the survivors. Polisario rejected categorically any new "Moroccan" shaikhs, partly because they would be receiving an allowance from the government and were therefore "under instructions," and partly because they could not possibly know the Sahrawis living in the camps. Polisario had an unstated difficulty of its own, the fact that SADR policy was to transcend a tribal society with tribespeople in the camps deliberately intermingled and not grouped as they would traditionally have been by subfraction. The shaikhs, who had been in some danger of marginalization, emerged with a new sense of power.

In spite of the modest progress achieved, the Secretary-General's report to the Security Council of 10 March 1994 reflected increasing pessimism. The Secretary-General announced the proposed withdrawal from MINURSO of the Australian signals contingent, the Canadian movement control unit and military observers as well as the Swiss medical unit, and he admitted that prospects for reconciling the opposed positions of the parties looked bleak.[13] Yaqub-Khan had few illusions and, as he said to me, felt the time had come for an "elegant exit." The king had told him he saw little point in pursuing talks with Polisario at this juncture, given the Polisario attitude; identification still seemed unlikely ever to happen. Yaqub-Khan departed for Pakistan later in the month and was not again involved with the work of the mission, although Boutros-Ghali, for political reasons of his own, kept his name on the books.

* * *

The Council was once more faced with a choice between three options, not altogether new. Under option A, the Council would decide to proceed with holding a referendum regardless of the cooperation of either party; under option B, the Identification Commission would continue its work for a prescribed time while the UN tried to obtain the cooperation of both parties, and at the end of the prescribed period the Council would review progress and decide on further action; under option C, the Council would conclude that the cooperation of both parties in the completion of the registration and identification process could not be obtained and decide that MINURSO would be either phased out or reduced to a military presence to encourage respect for the cease-fire.[14] The cost estimates submitted on 21 March might be seen as implying a bias toward decisive action—either option A or option C.[15] However, in its unanimous resolution of 31 March the Council opted for option B, without mention of the second phrase.[16]

After the departure of Yaqub-Khan, my position as head of mission was formalized, allowing me greater authority in discussion with the parties. I endeavored to persuade the Polisario leaders that they could have confidence in the identification procedure, that they would not be swamped by unqualified persons, and that any impostor would be exposed—which was a real concern to them. They were assured of a presence throughout: their observers as well as a shaikh from their side. April was a month of intensive negotiation in the camps near Tindouf, where every detail of the procedure was again and again meticulously rehearsed, and to an extent in Rabat. Morocco continued to express its readiness to proceed, but always on condition that the Perez de Cuellar criteria be explicitly accepted by Polisario and fully applied and that applications from persons in the census and those not included in the 1974 census be handled without distinction.

* * *

Morocco, I suspect, did not foresee that Polisario would agree to the 19 December criteria. It is possible that the Moroccans were still counting on Polisario's rejection, which would provide the Security Council with a compelling argument to revert to the option to proceed on one side alone and without the cooperation of the other party, as had been suggested again in the latest report. It astonished Rabat when, in late April, I communicated that the Polisario had accepted to begin in accordance with the criteria and that identification could proceed as recommended by Perez de Cuellar and welcomed by the Council. Basri wanted to see it in writing. The Frente Polisario confirmed its commitment in a letter to me dated 30 April, replying to mine of 27 April addressed, in identical terms, to both parties. On 20 May, King Hassan, in a letter to the Secretary-General, reiterated his country's respect for the deadlines set by the Council.[17]

Morocco undertook to open additional centers for registration in different parts of Laayoune and at the three other towns in the territory: Boujdour, Dakhla, and Smara. Mauritania concurred with our opening offices for registration at Nouadhibou and Zouerate. In the month of May, completed application forms began to be delivered to MINURSO, enabling the commission to analyze the data and prepare for identification. By early July, some 55,000 forms had been returned from the territory of Western Sahara, over 18,000 from the camps, and 3,000 from Zouerate. On 27 May I was received in audience by King Hassan. I told him that I saw identification as an important step forward but that the ultimate act of self-determination could most realistically be achieved through a politically negotiated settlement—a view he did not dismiss.

The procedural details of identification were yet again spelled out to the parties. After being photographed and fingerprinted, each applicant would appear before the Identification Commission team, in the presence of official observers from both sides and the OAU, to be questioned concerning his or her personal identity, tribal affiliation, and claims for eligibility to vote. The applicant would be asked to produce any supporting documentation, in the original—Polisario objected to photocopies—and the shaikhs, one from each side, would have the opportunity to examine such documents. The shaikhs, who, it was emphasized, would be required to take an oath swearing to the truthfulness of their testimony, were to be asked after every interview to sign a statement summarizing the testimony given. The Identification Commission would review all evidence and testimony provided at the identification session and undertake meticulous cross-referencing to the status of other family members, which could be completed only when all applicants from a given tribal subfraction had been identified.

Members of the Identification Commission and support staff were trained through simulation exercises and some technical problems were resolved before the launch of identification was announced on 1 June 1994, after Morocco and the Polisario had agreed on the subfractions with which to start and on the relevant shaikhs.[18] Detailed arrangements were negotiated for the security, travel, and accommodation of the shaikhs and the observers. An exchange of letters with the government of Morocco, the Frente Polisario, and the government of Algeria confirmed that in the performance of their duties, the shaikhs and the observers of the two parties were accorded immunities and privileges. Nothing could be taken for granted. Despite the cease-fire, the Frente Polisario and Morocco were in a state of war. In an atmosphere of general suspicion and profound mutual mistrust, the prospect of dispatching vulnerable, distinguished individuals into an "enemy" camp was a matter of genuine concern. Reciprocity offered some guarantee: it was organized that both sides would have an equivalent presence on the other. At the practical level, accommodation and food would be provided by the hosts to the best of their ability, but, at least at first, security was the paramount consideration. The solution lay in having UN aircraft (the appallingly uncomfortable troop-transporting Antonov, which we all had to use) depart simultaneously from Laayoune and Tindouf; by crossing midway in the air, each offered the assurance of hostages to the other side.

No sooner were we over the last hurdle to identification when another presented itself. According to the settlement proposals, the referendum was to be organized by the UN "in cooperation with OAU," and OAU representatives were to be associated with the process throughout as official observers.[19] Already, in May 1993, the then chairman of the OAU, President Abdou Diouf of Senegal, had been invited to appoint two representatives, and these had been named. On 19 August, in an official communication, the Moroccan minister for foreign affairs noted that the OAU observers had been "designated from among officials of the secretariat of an organization which, in admitting the 'pseudo SADR' as a member had already prejudged the outcome of the referendum."[20] (Morocco's ambassador to the UN, Ahmed Snoussi, reaffirmed: "We consider that the OAU has been creating an illegal, illegitimate situation. Recognizing people that have no flag or territory is a clear violation of the OAU charter."[21]) Morocco would "acquiesce in the participation of the OAU only if the latter adopted 'a rational position with regard to the right of the populations of Western Sahara for self-determination, by at least suspending the participation of the "pseudo SADR" in the activities of the OAU.'"[22] The minister added that Morocco would not object to the designation by the president of Egypt, as current chairman of the OAU, of personal representatives to follow the work of the Identification Commission.

By June 1994 the issue had still to be resolved. On 17 June, the Secretary-General decided to write directly to the OAU chairman and its secretary-general. He invited President Ben Ali of Tunisia, the year's chairman of the OAU, to designate his representatives, stressing that "at this crucial stage in the process, the continued cooperation and support of OAU" was more important than ever to the success of the operation.[23] In early July, Boutros Boutros-Ghali followed up with a further letter, this time addressed to the Tunisian minister for foreign affairs, requesting a speedy settlement of the problem.[24]

Without an OAU presence there could be no question of starting; on that the Polisario was adamant. We adjusted the timetable—again. Then, on 23 July, the Secretary-General received a letter from the president of Tunisia providing a "unique and indivisible" list of four observers, comprising the two observers previously designated and two others.[25] It was not easy for the Moroccans to swallow, but they accepted; President Ben Ali was a friend. We prepared to begin, only to be informed that one of the designated observers would not be available after all; his replacement should not be expected until sometime in August. The parties were determined to await all four observers on the "unique and indivisible" list. The fourth man finally arrived toward the end of the month, and all four traveled together to Laayoune.

On 28 August 1994 the identification process was successfully launched with simultaneous ceremonies in Laayoune and at the El-Aiun camp near Tindouf, attended by Moroccan dignitaries on one side and Polisario on the other. The first three days exceeded all expectation considering the novelty of the proceedings, the heavy air of suspicion with which each side viewed the other, and the complex administration involved. A last-minute crisis was averted when one side provided the name of the wrong shaikh and the other reacted as if to a case of criminal deception, only to discover that it had been a genuine transmission error with two similar names inadvertently transposed. The shaikhs emerged in time for their flights and, accompanied by the official observers, crossed in midair the flight path of those traveling in the opposite direction. Practical aspects, including escort arrangements, went according to plan. The only hitch had to do with the party representatives' ability to communicate with their respective authorities; it was resolved with practical help from MINURSO. The machinery had begun to function. Then, after three days, the promising start had to be put on hold. Identification was temporarily suspended on 1 September, when one of the OAU's designated observers departed to meet a prior commitment elsewhere. It resumed on 21 September after his replacement had appeared.

The OAU observers generated another problem: how they should be described in the identification chamber. Morocco categorically refused to have name plates inscribed "OAU" on the grounds that the observers had been personally designated by the Tunisian president, as current OAU chairman, and they were not representatives of the organization as such. Polisario insisted that they should be clearly identified as representing the OAU, in a manner similar to the name plates marking the representatives of the two parties. Compromise was elusive until the OAU observers agreed to sport prominently in their buttonhole the OAU emblem and both sides accepted—with equal lack of enthusiasm.

On 21 September, on the resumption of identification, I addressed a letter to Morocco and the Polisario setting 15 October as the closing date for the receipt of applications.[26] Then, on 8–9 October, a freakish rainstorm swept through the Tindouf region, causing extraordinary flash flooding. One of the refugee camps, with housing made of tent cloth and compacted mud bricks, virtually dissolved; a child and an old woman were drowned. Extensive damage and disruption affected the whole district, which for days resembled a vast lake until the waters seeped into the rocky desert floor. I declared a ten-day extension of the deadline.

By midnight on the day of the deadline, the Polisario had submitted 42,468 application forms, and Morocco, at the very last minute, hoping first to know how many Polisario had produced, sent in 176,533 for the territory and beyond; the Secretary-General's report referred to "a flood."[27] The overall total came eventually to 233,487, with the 14,486 presented in Mauritania.[28] Some 4,000 potential voters were already through the identification process. Although the number of identification centers had been increased and more were planned, it was immediately obvious that the enormous number of applications received, far exceeding the total of persons in the census, would require many long weeks to process and many months to identify. The practical problem created by the volume of applications was not the only difficulty. Polisario saw it as evidence of Morocco's duplicitous intentions and became more determined than ever not to be bulldozed beyond its principled position regarding those listed in the 1974 census.

Notes

1. Colonel Cuevas served as a consultant to MINURSO in the summer of 1993. See also Report of the Secretary-General, S/23299 (19 December 1991), Annex IV, par. 15.

2. Notably the founder and first secretary-general El-Ouali, elder brother of Mustapha Bachir Sayed, and Mohamed Abdel-Aziz, who became secretary-general after the death of El-Ouali.

3. Conversation in a Polisario camp.

4. Report of the Secretary-General, S/23299 (19 December 1991), Annex III, par. 10.

5. Ibid., Annex VII, par. 21.

6. Ibid., Annex IV, par. 14.

7. Security Council Resolution 809(1993), 2 March 1993.

8. Ibid., operative par. 3.

9. Ibid., preambular par. 6 and operative par. 5.

10. Report of the Secretary-General, S/23662 (28 February 1992), par. 32: "The United Nations has never before organized a referendum of this kind."

11. Letter dated 28 September 1993.

12. Report of the Secretary-General, S/26797 (24 November 1993), par. 28.

13. Report of the Secretary-General, S/1994/283 (10 March 1994), par. 7.

14. Ibid., pars. 24–26.

15. Ibid., Addendum.

16. Security Council Resolution 907(1994), 31 March 1994.

17. Report of the Secretary-General, S/1994/819 (12 July 1994), par. 16.

18. See ibid., par. 26.

19. Ibid., par. 28, referring to Report of the Secretary-General, S/21360 (18 June 1990), pars. 26, 39, 46.

20. Ibid., par. 30.

21. Adekeye Adebajo, "Selling Out the Sahara: The Tragic Tale of the UN Referendum," Cornell University, Institute for African Development, Occasional Papers Series, Spring 2002, 12.

22. Report of the Secretary-General, S/1994/819 (12 July 1994), par. 30.

23. Ibid., par. 32.

24. Ibid.

25. Report of the Secretary-General, S/1994/1257 (5 November 1994), par. 9.

26. Ibid., par. 14.

27. Ibid., par. 15.

28. Report of the Secretary-General, S/1995/986 (24 November 1995), par. 12.

6

The Process Stalls

In the weeks that followed, all the difficulties that were to beset the identification process became apparent. Morocco wanted to ensure that Polisario did not finish first: it was concerned lest all those included in the census be completed ahead of identification of the many applicants not in the census, more specifically those from the three contested tribal groups. The battle of reciprocity had begun. The presence of the shaikhs was essential, which meant that work had to be suspended whenever either side had difficulty in making its shaikh available or, preferring to delay, had its shaikh fail to arrive, arrive late, or leave early. This was in addition to the natural hazards of desert life: the shaikh who accidentally missed his scheduled flight—bound to occur occasionally with the severely limited communications available in and around the camps—and cases of genuine sickness. Everything, sickness included, became subject to a political interpretation, as partisan, an unacceptable obstacle to identification, and turned into a reason for suspending work elsewhere. Insistence on strict reciprocity implied that whenever, for whatever reason, identification could not take place at one center, work was automatically suspended at a center on the other side.[1] Even the target figure proposed for identification, 150 persons at each center each day, was transformed into a maximum by the parties' anxiety to control the process. They exploited the shaikhs' presence and absence to make certain that the UN Identification Commission complied.

Boutros Boutros-Ghali visited the region toward the end of November 1994. I joined him in Algiers, at the sumptuous government guest hotel overlooking the bay. He suggested we talk in the garden; it would be more discreet. I began by telling him the current unkind joke about Basri: King Hassan had had a call from his friend Mobutu Sese Seko (still running Zaire) to say that he was planning a democratic election and needed help; apparently Hassan had a man who was excellent at organizing such things, and could he assist? Hassan duly dispatched Basri and was startled when, shortly after the election, Mobutu called not to thank him but to complain. Hassan summoned Basri, who sounded surprised; he thought the election had been a huge success when 99 percent voted for King Hassan.

Boutros-Ghali was amused. He knew only too well all the personalities involved. The Western Sahara issue had been a responsibility of his as deputy prime minister for foreign affairs of Egypt and before that for more than a decade as minister of state for foreign affairs, and he had been deeply involved in the OAU controversy over SADR's membership. He was easy to brief.

I had prepared a note: one side of one page, as Winston Churchill prescribed. My strategy was to get the process going but with no illusion that the parties would cooperate in implementing entirely the settlement plan as it stood. I hoped that engaging both Morocco and the Polisario for long enough and for them to see where they were headed would induce them to talk. A realistic solution to the conflict would require a politically negotiated compromise to be endorsed in an act of self-determination. The Secretary-General agreed. He said he had no need to keep a copy of the written brief.

At that moment he was called urgently to the telephone. He was deeply embroiled in the dispute about air strikes in Bosnia. The U.S. ambassador to the UN, Madeleine Albright, also telephoned him in Morocco, and on 30 November he went to Sarajevo to warn that the UN force would withdraw unless a countrywide cease-fire was established.[2] These events had no direct bearing on Western Sahara, but the personalities and their personality conflicts—there was limited sympathy between Boutros-Ghali and Albright—came to have repercussions. Boutros-Ghali was well aware that in the U.S. congressional elections of 1994 the ultra-conservative right under Newt Gingrich had achieved broad support and contributed to a groundswell of anti-UN feeling in Washington. The Secretary-General alerted me to the increasing U.S. disenchantment with costly peacekeeping missions and warned about the repeated interruptions and delays to which identification was subject. There had been a sea change in Security Council thinking spearheaded by the United States and a new willingness to concede lack of success and to terminate a mission—he quoted Somalia as an example—or at least to reduce it to symbolic proportions. Cyprus and the former Yugoslavia were exceptions because they mattered to *les grands* in a way that Western Sahara did not.

During the months following, as part of efforts to discredit the UN, the mission and I were criticized largely for failing to take a tough stance against what one right-wing U.S. critic called Moroccan "gangsterism."[3] There was Moroccan heavy-handedness, to be sure, but what was interesting about this criticism was how a politically experienced operator chose to miss the point. It was not only that we depended, as always, on the parties' willing cooperation, since we had no powers of coercion under the "court of world opinion"—the Security Council never so much as whispered the word *sanction*—but, equally important, Morocco was unlikely to be perturbed by any threat of stopping the process; the challenge was to keep it engaged. Our objective was to stay on course, to handle the maneuvering of both sides, not to provide either with any pretext to withdraw or excuse to scuttle the process, so long as the mission's credibility was not convincingly challenged, and thus to maintain sufficient progress through the critical early stages. We needed to keep the settlement plan in gear, albeit low gear, for long enough to convince both parties and the outside world that identification should be a stepping-stone to self-determination by way of a negotiated agreement within or outside the settlement plan.

Western Sahara:
MINURSO Deployment, March 1995

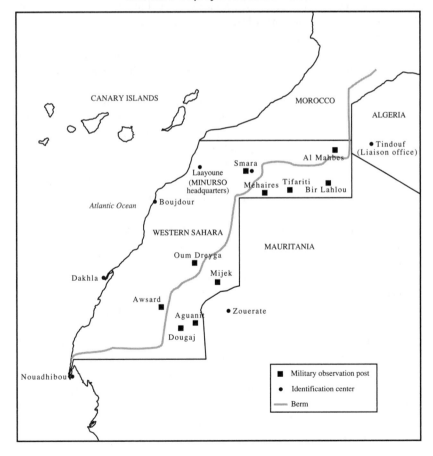

Identification, having begun at two centers, expanded during the autumn of 1994 to four centers, and two further centers opened in February 1995, at Smara and in the camps. By 9 March, there was a seventh at Dakhla, the only town in the southern part of Western Sahara, and arrangements were well advanced to open an eighth center at Polisario's Dakhla camp, which was sited some 180 kilometers from Tindouf and presented manifold logistical problems. It helped when Algeria gave its agreement to helicopter overflights.

As identification advanced, the problem of missing shaikhs started to close in. Even balance between the two sides, helpful though it was, did not resolve the difficulty of how to replace the shaikhs for one-third of the agreed-upon eighty-eight subfractions. Morocco continued to argue that the shaikhs chosen in 1973 had been elected for a five-year term and that there was no logic in insisting that only shaikhs of the 1973 election were acceptable. Polisario refused point-blank to regard as valid the many shaikhs who had been appointed on the Moroccan side since 1973. That identification related to the period before the Sahrawis found themselves divided reinforced Polisario's argument. Morocco, initially reluctant, eventually conceded that the 1973 shaikh election should provide the point of reference.

But how to select replacement shaikhs from thirty-odd subfractions for their indispensable role in identification? Although there was no automatic right of succession in Sahrawi tribal practice, Polisario argued that an eldest son could replace his dead father. Morocco said no. Only as both sides worked laboriously through their records and checked the prospective candidates could they be brought to accept the eldest son principle. There were still subfractions where the deceased shaikh had no son. It took ingenuity to develop a formula potentially acceptable to both parties: the solution was to accept as shaikh a surviving nonelected candidate from the 1973 election, with priority to the one who had received most votes. That the nonelected should be chosen seemed curious only until it was understood that the short-listed candidates were all eminent elders, notables of their tribal group. Isolated cases remained where there was no surviving shaikh, son, or even candidate. My compromise was to have three names put forward of respected members of the subfraction from which the other side would choose, and failing a decision on their part or if they stalled, the chairman of the Identification Commission would decide. The last was not ideal, and it did give rise to difficulty, but the formula as a whole worked and enabled identification to proceed. Both Polisario and Morocco knew that the crunch would come when they were called upon to identify the large tribal groupings, in particular that of "northern tribes," encompassing numerous subfractions for which the Polisario had neither shaikhs nor notables—and in some cases no individuals to propose.

By mid-March 1995, over 21,300 persons had been identified. Progress since the beginning of the year had been steady and incremental. There were modest signs that suspicion and mistrust were waning; emotional reunions were common at identification sessions, though it was perhaps tempting to invest more political significance in them than was warranted. Transfer flights from one side to the other were becoming routine; both Morocco and Polisario were noticeably less obsessive about security. (On the other hand, complaints increased about life in the camps for the Moroccan team on duty: there was consternation that a fastidious observer, not a goat eater, should have to survive on a week's ration of tough goat meat!) But insistence on reciprocity was the major impediment. The Secretary-General, in his 30 March 1995 report to the Security Council, urged both parties "to abandon any insistence on strict reciprocity in the number of centers and on the linkage of a center on one side with a specific center on the other, since the distribution of population is uneven." He went on: "Nor should limits be imposed on the numbers to be identified on any given day. There should be no reluctance to permit the process to advance more expeditiously in one place than the other."[4]

The identification of persons whose names appeared on the revised census list was, as always, straightforward. The individual had only to present his or her (Spanish) documentation and have his or her personal identity confirmed by the shaikh. This served the Polisario throughout: the candidates they wished to be found eligible were readily processed. In the camps that applied to the overwhelming majority, and even in the territory there were considerable numbers who had been included in the census. The problem for Morocco related to applicants not on the revised list who based their claim on one or another of the contentious eligibility criteria, who were without acceptable documents and relied on oral testimony to prove their case. This took time. The shaikhs, with their newfound power, flaunted their right to ask probing questions and refused to be rushed. Morocco was increasingly anxious about the likelihood of arriving at a point where virtually all the candidates from the census had been identified while most of the others still remained to be processed. Given the relative numbers, it was almost inevitable that all applicants would be finished in the camps long before identification was completed in the territory.

Even with eight centers operational, including that at the Dakhla camp in the Tindouf area, which posed huge logistical challenges for ferrying personnel in and out as well as for their sustenance, the rate of identification was uneven. In March and early April, severe sandstorms grounded aircraft. The presence of shaikhs was subject to the vagaries of desert life as well as party control. The compromise on substitute shaikhs worked most of the time, but there was a quibble about one provision. The Moroccans wanted a flexible interpretation of "eldest" son in circumstances where the eldest was not deemed mentally fit; Polisario stayed restrictive. Both sides were irredeemably suspicious of any case where a shaikh was declared unfit or unavailable for any reason and attributed that to manipulation by the other party. Morocco and Polisario always seemed to know what transpired on the other side and would explain to me the duplicitous reasons given by the other in order to ensure a compliant shaikh.

By the middle of May, although the process stumbled and occasionally stalled, 35,851 persons had been identified. At MINURSO headquarters all the information from the identification sessions, documentary evidence provided and testimony given, was data processed and meticulously scrutinized to ensure compatibility and prevent duplication. This revealed a few anomalies. It was essential to reconcile findings so as to be certain that siblings and other relatives benefited from similar treatment. Since the review process could not be definitively completed until all candidates from a given subfraction had been identified, it was impossible to release figures meanwhile for those found eligible. That led to accusations of insufficient transparency, but my principal concern was to be sure that when the results were published there need be no subsequent retraction or change. Unfortunately, an imaginative and independent-minded Identification Commission member in charge of the review process referred to it as "legal review," implying a dimension that this technical operation was not designed to have. This gave rise to unnecessary misconceptions and compounded suspicion.

The Secretary-General's appeal for the "atmosphere of trust and serenity" essential for the commission to carry out its task and his affirmation that "the process cannot be brought to a successful conclusion without the full cooperation of the parties" failed to convince.[5] Demonstrations in Laayoune on 11 May 1995 resulted in the arrest of young Sahrawis. The Security Council, in the meantime, concerned at the practices that were hampering progress, frustrated by the constant delays to the settlement plan, and under pressure to cut costs, decided to send a special mission to the region. The mission, composed of ambassadors from Argentina, Botswana, Honduras, Oman, and the United States and the representative of France, visited Morocco, Algeria, and Mauritania from 3 to 9 June for meetings with Moroccan, Algerian, and Mauritanian government ministers and officials and with the Polisario leaders. The Council members were in hortatory mood. They urged both sides to abandon insistence on reciprocity in the number and operation of centers, to refrain from blaming the other side, to lift the limit on the number to be identified in any one day, and to expedite the review of undecided cases. They also called on Morocco to conduct a preliminary vetting of the 100,000 applicants residing outside the territory, since during the mission Morocco had announced its intention to present these for identification. The Council mission also recommended the start of identification operations in Mauritania.[6]

Barely had the ambassadors returned to New York when, on 21 June, the young demonstrators were sentenced. Eight of them, civilians, received prison terms of fifteen to twenty years for having participated in a rally to promote Western Saharan independence. The Frente Polisario at once informed the president of the Security Council of its decision to suspend participation in the process and to recall its observers, having been incensed already by the Moroccan decision to present the 100,000 "Moroccan settlers" for identification.[7] The Polisario demanded the immediate release of political prisoners arrested since the deployment of MINURSO, specifically the eight just sentenced, and an end to the moving of "foreigners" into the territory. Such action, according to Polisario, was necessary to restore credibility in the process. Morocco responded on 26 June that it was not for the other party to decide on the true identity of an applicant before the Identification Commission reached its decision on the basis of the established criteria, regardless of whether the person lived in or outside the territory. Nor was Morocco prepared to accept indefinite postponement of the proceedings.[8]

By royal edict on 9 July, on the occasion of the king's birthday, the prison sentences of the eight Saharan civilians were commuted to one year.[9] On 12 July the Polisario agreed to resume identification. That same day Abdel-Aziz, in a communication to the Security Council president, reiterated Polisario's view that "the 1974 census constitutes the only basis recognized in the settlement plan as accepted by the two parties and endorsed by the United Nations." The participation of a "substitute population, sought by the occupying Power, whose most recent maneuver was the attempt to include 100,000 of its nationals in the voters' list," was unacceptable.[10]

Identification resumed, the substantive review of specific cases continued, and arrangements were finalized to open identification centers at Nouadhibou and Zouerate in Mauritania. But the identification process remained subject to just as many difficulties as before. Though halts and hiccups failed to stop the processing of applicants included in the revised census list, which proceeded correctly, those not listed, who relied on oral testimony, ideally the concurring testimony of both shaikhs, made for hard going. It was becoming increasingly apparent that not all shaikhs were independent nobles as heralded; their political instincts had been nurtured, and they had discovered the power of exercising a negative vote to veto unwanted applicants.

The shaikh problem manifested itself with new force when it came to detailed planning for the identification of the very large numbers from the three tribal groupings that Polisario hotly contested. Whereas surviving shaikhs from the 1973 election and the substitute formula covered all subfractions belonging to the seven main tribes, the three tribal groupings were a different issue. Morocco insisted that all ten "tribes," as categorized in the 1974 census, merited identical treatment. The Polisario was equally adamant that the last three were not tribes composed of subfractions, that the Polisario did not have shaikhs for these groups or even notables, and that, in any event, the vast number of applicants made a mockery of an identification procedure based on shaikhs' personal knowledge of their people. Neither argument was entirely valid. There was no doubt that census categories A through G (they were listed under alphabetical heads) were Sahrawi tribes and that the majority of their subfractions inhabited Western Sahara. Categories H, I, and J also included Saharans and comprised individuals who were living, employed, or married in Spanish Sahara at the time of the census. Most of these indeed belonged to Sahrawi tribes, but tribes whose traditional domain lay mainly outside the territory and were predominantly associated with neighboring countries, especially Morocco and Mauritania. H, the eighth group, which was the most contentious, lumped under one head a collection of tribes "from the north" and thus a miscellany of individuals having tribal links with the Western Sahara border area with Morocco and beyond. H included such major tribes as the Ait Ousa as well as persons from the Rif in the northernmost region of the kingdom, which had been under Spanish protection. Also involved was the Ait Baamran, an important Saharan tribal federation with members living over a large area, whose heartland was at Sidi Ifni, the Spanish colonial enclave north of Western Sahara that had been restored to Morocco in 1969. The ninth grouping, I, comprised Chorfa tribes claiming descent from the prophet Muhammad. The tenth group, J, brought together persons from various coastal tribes and tribes "of the south," largely associated with Mauritania. Under Spanish administration, shaikhs had been attributed to these groupings, but they could hardly be expected to be familiar with or know about, let alone recognize, the great majority of tribal members and others living elsewhere.

It must have been a matter of ever increasing concern to Morocco that the identification of nearly all those included in the 1974 census would be completed long before serious identification of the many applicants from these contested groups was advanced. In early August Morocco's minister of interior announced its readiness to open forty new identification centers outside the territory to speed up the process, a proposal entirely unacceptable to Polisario.[11] On 7 August Polisario conveyed its decision to refuse participation, until certain conditions had been met, in identifying applicants from the Chorfa as well as the groupings of "Northern Tribes" and "Coastal and Southern Tribes."[12] A suggestion that we leave the contested till last met with a categorical rebuttal from the Moroccans. Morocco rejected "excessive reliance on the 1974 census"; all should be treated equally, and there could be no hierarchy of criteria. Identification was being ground to a standstill.

In the autumn of 1995, we made two concerted attempts to resolve the crisis. Without the cooperation of both parties, progress was impossible, and the first formula was intended to pressure them into cooperating. The core problem was to devise a way of identifying applicants from the groups for which there was no qualified shaikh or alternate who could be made available on the Polisario side. The proposal was that identification would continue as before for the eighty-eight subfractions for which a shaikh or alternate had been accepted in principle, *but* identification could proceed with candidates from other groups, in the territory or outside, in the presence of two shaikhs from the tribal group concerned, not necessarily one from each side. For the procedure to command credibility in the absence of a shaikh from the Polisario side, documentary evidence would be required: a birth certificate to prove that the applicant was born of a Saharan father and supporting evidence of the father's birth in the territory. The Frente Polisario would, of course, be invited, and expected, to observe the proceedings and to make any views known in accordance with the established procedures. The presence of the OAU observers provided a further reassuring element.[13]

On 10 October 1995 the Secretary-General met in New York with an impressive Moroccan delegation led by Driss Slaoui, counselor to the king and former ambassador; Driss Basri, minister of interior; General Housni Bensliman, commandant of the Royal Gendarmerie; Morrocan ambassador to the UN Ahmed Snoussi; and Governor Mohammed Azmi.[14] The Moroccans listened attentively to the proposal, and there was a sense that they might accept. On my return to the region, I met with Ali Beiba, "prime minister" of the SADR. In a follow-up letter dated 26 October, he assured me of Polisario's willingness to cooperate with the Secretary-General's proposed program to identify all applicants in the territory and outside, in the camps, the Tindouf region, and Mauritania, "in conformity with the settlement plan."[15]

On 27 October the Secretary-General addressed a letter to the president of the Security Council in which he took the suggested course of action a step further. He explained that identification would proceed unchanged for applicants from the eighty-eight subfractions for which there was a shaikh or alternate on both sides; however, identification could take place even in the absence of a party representative, shaikh, or OAU observer provided that the identification schedule had been duly communicated to the parties, the convocation lists had been issued in correct time, and hours of work had been announced. As for the three tribal groupings, he spelled out that in addition to showing a birth certificate giving the father's name, the applicant would be required to produce documentation issued before 1976 by the competent authorities within Western Sahara's recognized frontiers substantiating the father's birth in the territory.[16]

Morocco said no. In communications to me of 25 and 29 October, Basri argued that the change as proposed would be "prejudicial to the inalienable rights of Western Saharans to equal treatment by the Identification Commission and to the interests of Morocco."[17] In Morocco's view, the difference in treatment between members of the eighty-eight subfractions and other applicants amounted to discrimination and was contrary to the settlement plan. It constituted a radical departure from the plan and the instructions given to the Identification Commission, which recognized the particular nature of Saharan society and the role of oral testimony alongside documentary evidence. Morocco also had reservations regarding documents issued by the Spanish colonial administration.

In November, there was a penultimate attempt to keep identification alive. There would be no distinction as such between the seven tribes and the three tribal groupings. All would be treated in accordance with established practice. Both sides, as before, would be asked to provide representatives and to present a shaikh or alternate, and the OAU was expected to send observers. However, if and when one party did not for any reason provide a shaikh or someone to function in his place, identification could still take place with the participation of one side only on the basis of appropriate documentation, with the assistance of the one shaikh present. Were neither party able or willing to make a shaikh available, identification would be based on documentary evidence only.[18] The intention, of course, was to cajole both sides into providing persons to fill the shaikh's role.

Morocco again wished to be assured that the shaikh, when only one was present, would contribute to identification in exactly the same manner as when there were two, and again it stressed the "privileged" place of oral testimony.[19] Since Morocco had already rejected all attempts to restrict valid documents to those issued by the Spanish authorities, reference to appropriate documentation was considered too vague and therefore liable to a restrictive interpretation. Morocco dismissed as unacceptable the suggestion that identification could occur without the participation of any shaikh, since that would exclude oral testimony entirely.

Polisario spokesmen also refused. They construed the proposal as a reversal of the earlier approach, which they criticized Morocco for having rejected.[20] The secretary-general of the Frente Polisario restated their position in a letter dated 18 November. The Frente Polisario had not been consulted in the formulation of the eligibility criteria, and its concerns had not been taken into account in the compromise concerning the application and interpretation of the criteria. The latest proposal would again give Morocco an added advantage and the opportunity to introduce, by means of its chosen shaikh or its own documents, 135,000 applicants who had no ties with Western Sahara. This would be tantamount to holding a referendum for a people other than the Western Saharans.

As a final token gesture, the UN Secretary-General suggested that identification of applicants from the contested groups might proceed following the established procedure but if necessary with the presence of one side only, though "both parties would be invited to provide sheikhs and representatives" and "it is my hope that both would be represented even in circumstances when they do not provide a sheikh." It would be "up to the Identification Commission to determine the validity of the oral testimony and of the documentary evidence and to decide on the merits of each applicant."[21] He did not expect a warm welcome, nor did he receive one. The Polisario were irate and held me responsible for trying to skew the process against them, when what had been intended was to oblige them to safeguard their interests by being present.

It could be said that every avenue had been explored. No stone was left unturned to further the identification process with the voluntary cooperation of both parties.

The Security Council reacted unenthusiastically to the Secretary-General's late November report. While welcoming the Secretary-General's efforts, the Council requested the Secretary-General, in the event that his consultations failed to reach agreement, "to provide the Council with options for its consideration, including a programme for the orderly withdrawal of the UN mission for the referendum in Western Sahara."[22] Explicit was U.S. pressure to reduce peacekeeping costs, to "spool in" a mission in which U.S. interests were not actively engaged and which showed few signs of coming to early closure.

During consultations, the informal closed meetings of Security Council members that precede decisions or debate in open session, and of which no official records are maintained, Boutros-Ghali had himself admitted that the difference between the two sides was irreconcilable and could not be overcome by changing procedures. It shocked some members when he went on to concede that although he had hoped to see identification completed, he had not really expected the referendum as envisioned in the settlement plan to prove possible. His hope had been that faced with the figures emerging from identification, the parties would start direct negotiations.[23]

* * *

That same month the General Assembly, while reiterating support for the settlement plan, once more called on the parties to cooperate and expressed the hope that direct talks would soon resume.[24] The Secretary-General, while preparing the ground for a possible reduction of MINURSO and eventual withdrawal, chose to dispatch as special envoy Chinmaya Garekhan, an undersecretary general and adviser to the Secretary-General. Garekhan visited the region from 2 to 9 January 1996.

Morocco and the Frente Polisario yet again "confirmed their commitment and continuing desire to hold a free and fair referendum on the future status of Western Sahara in conformity with the settlement plan." They assured Garekhan of "their readiness to cooperate fully with the UN in order to overcome the obstacles standing in the way of the implementation of the plan. At the same time, each of the parties insisted that there was no room left for additional concessions on its part. Consequently, each party stressed that progress was contingent on the readiness of the other party to adjust its position as required."[25] There was little sense of flexibility, let alone any real change of position regarding identification. Morocco continued to emphasize that every applicant had to be identified and that all forms of evidence, whether documentary proof or oral testimony, carried equal weight. Polisario said it would be willing to participate in identifying any applicant from a subfraction represented in the 1974 census but rejected the three tribal groupings—most especially the "subfractional" entities classified as H41, H61, and J51/52—as inadmissible. What was more, it was unable to present shaikhs or alternates for these groups. The Frente Polisario was resolutely opposed to identification's taking place with the participation of a shaikh from one side only; were that to happen it would feel compelled to withdraw from the entire process. The Polisario strongly favored talks; Morocco, while not convinced that dialogue at this stage would serve much purpose and believing that it might even complicate the situation, was not totally opposed to talks, whether direct or indirect.

Reporting to the Secretary-General, Garekhan rejected allegations impugning the integrity of individual Identification Commission members; the commission's work was not made easier by the parties' critical scrutiny. He concluded that increased "transparency" could contribute to reducing mistrust and suspicion and wanted the Identification Commission to share with the parties lists of applicants already identified and found eligible to vote, as well as a list of applicants awaiting identification.[26]

To share the list of persons still to be identified posed no problem in principle. In a sense it was already being done, as names were provided to both sides on an ongoing basis in good time prior to identification. A comprehensive listing would be a bulky undertaking and technically demanding but carried no other implications than the fury that the many applicants would cause the Polisario and, inevitably, a sprinkling of errors in names and other facts. Lists of persons found eligible to vote were another matter. The meticulous review process that was under way could be finalized only when all the applicants from any one subfraction had been identified, wherever they happened to be processed, in the territory, the camps, Mauritania, or beyond. The procedure involved thorough cross-referencing. I was determined to avoid the inclusion or omission of names that the Identification Commission would later have to retract or insert (such an occurrance did precipitate a crisis years later).

There was also another concern. I believed that the unrelieved close scrutiny of all commission members by both sides and the copious records that the party representatives compiled at every session would make it all too easy to establish which commission member had influenced which decision. Not all commission members could be expected to be equally resistant to the intense pressure, or inducements, to which they might be made subject. As it was, from observation of identification proceedings, the testimony offered, and the shaikhs' intervention, both Morocco and the Frente Polisario, with their representatives present throughout, knew sufficiently well what the verdict was likely to be. All that occurred at every session was transparent, even embarrassingly so.

Immediately after the adoption of Resolution 1042[27] by the Security Council, following the Secretary-General's report submitted after Garekhan's visit, and given Morocco's and the Polisario's explicit recommitment to the settlement plan, a full and detailed identification program, based on established practice and beginning with the recognized tribes, was readied for submission to the parties. Morocco remonstrated against any differentiation in the treatment of tribal groups: the Moroccans were unwilling to postpone identification of the contested groups, maintaining that they were not party to any compromise on that subject. Furthermore, until all identification had been completed, they resolutely opposed the issuing of lists of persons found eligible to vote, contending that the disclosure of such lists would be an unacceptable departure from the plan and had not been approved by the Security Council. Despite the tensions of work during Ramadan, we hammered out a partial compromise. Identification would resume with applicants from the noncontested groups on the explicit understanding that from the fourth week, applicants from the contested groups would be included, and the most contentious (H41 and 61 and J51/52) would begin identification as of the seventh week. Meanwhile, there could be no disclosure of lists of persons found eligible. The Polisario, after discussion, accepted the program proposed for the first three weeks, but on condition that the lists of eligible persons were made available before the end of that period. Polisario refused to commit itself to participate in identifying applicants from any of the tribal groupings H through J, including the Chorfa in I. Identification stopped.

When identification halted, a grand total of 77,058 applicants had been convoked and 60,112 identified; roughly 75 percent of persons in the camps and 80 percent in the territory appeared when convoked. Given the revised census list number of 73,497, these were impressive figures, and the hearings had been quite sufficient to reveal to an initiate which way the wind was blowing.

Notes

1. Report of the Secretary-General, S/1995/240 (30 March 1995), par. 4.
2. Boutros Boutros-Ghali, *Unvanquished: A U.S.-U.N. Saga* (New York: Random House, 1999), 214.

3. *Washington Times,* 27 January 1999, repeating the accusation made by a former staff member in December 1994. His charges of mismanagement and "anti-Americanism" at MINURSO provoked a full investigation by the new Office of Internal Oversight Services. The auditors "concluded that the allegations had been triggered primarily by . . . frustration over non-extension of his contract and by personal animosity" (*Yearbook of the United Nations* [New York: UN Office of Public Information, 1994] 49: 261, summarizing UN document A/49/884).

4. Report of the Secretary-General, S/1995/240 (30 March 1995), par. 40.

5. Report of the Secretary-General, S/1995/404 (19 May 1995), par. 33, citing S/23299 (19 December 1991); also par. 37.

6. UN document S/1995/498 (21 June 1995).

7. UN document S/1995/524 (23 June 1995).

8. UN document S/1995/514 (26 June 1995).

9. See Report of the Secretary-General, S/1995/779 (8 September 1995), par. 6.

10. Ibid.

11. Ibid., par. 7.

12. Ibid., par. 9.

13. Ibid., par. 49.

14. Report of the Secretary-General, S/1995/986 (24 November 1995), par. 4.

15. Ibid., par. 5.

16. UN document S/1995/924 (27 October 1995), referred to in Report of the Secretary-General, S/1995/986 (24 November 1995), par. 4.

17. Report of the Secretary-General, S/1995/986 (24 November 1995), par. 6.

18. Ibid., par. 7.

19. Ibid., par. 10.

20. Ibid., par. 11.

21. Ibid., par. 16.

22. Security Council Resolution 1033(1995), 19 December 1995.

23. Personal communication and interview with Boutros Boutros-Ghali, Paris, April 2003.

24. General Assembly Resolution 50/36 (6 December 1995).

25. Report of the Secretary-General, S/1996/43 (19 January 1996), par. 6.

26. Ibid., pars. 10, 15, 16.

27. Security Council Resolution 1042(1996), 31 January 1996.

7

UN Settlement Efforts Renewed

In his 8 May 1996 report to the Security Council, Secretary-General Boutros Boutros-Ghali proposed that following suspension of the identification process, members of the Identification Commission should depart the mission, leaving only sufficient personnel to ensure orderly closure of the centers and the secure storage of identification data. The records of the Identification Commission would be transferred to the UN Office at Geneva for safekeeping. Boutros-Ghali recommended other reductions also: the withdrawal of almost the entire civilian police component, a 20 percent decrease in the military, and corresponding cuts in civilian support staff. He insisted, however, that the UN could not abandon its responsibility: "The international community must remain determined to see not only peace maintained in the region but every effort made for the people of Western Sahara to decide on their future status in a way that will bring lasting peace and stability." He therefore proposed to keep a small political office to "maintain a dialogue . . . and facilitate any other effort that could help set the parties on a course towards an agreed formula for the resolution of their differences."[1] The Council agreed.[2]

The departure of Identification Commission members and other staff was fraught with unpleasantness. Uniformed personnel from the civilian police and military returned to their national service, but many others had no alternative employment in sight. That a few were to remain exacerbated the pain of decision. Staffing problems have to be a feature of any long-lasting mission, and however competent the chief administrative officer—for much of my time with the mission I was fortunate in having the help of the experienced French-, English-, and Arabic-speaking Ali Ouni—the most intractable cases come to the head of mission, making major inroads on time and emotional energy. Simultaneously, I was exploring an equally intractable proposition that had been mooted every so often, the idea of reassembling the shaikhs. Like any identification-related initiative, it foundered on the irreconcilable positions of the parties, with Morocco ever adamant that there must be no distinction between the tribes (A through G) and the tribal groupings (H through J) and Polisario equally adamant in rejecting the three tribal groupings, for which, as always, it claimed not to have shaikhs.

My more hopeful aspirations lay elsewhere. It was vaguely thought, though not specifically articulated, that the reduction of the mission would help prompt dialogue. I knew that the United States was discreetly involved in undercover efforts to foster negotiation. I knew because one regular emissary relied on MINURSO flights from Laayoune to Tindouf, and the Polisario gave me more than hints regarding why he went to see them. Unfortunately, nothing came of the initiative, and in early summer, a U.S. State Department official let me understand that the field was open. Once it was clear that I was not competing, I moved on my own account to explore whether the time might be ripe for a serious encounter between Morocco and the Frente Polisario. I embarked on a sequence of meetings, increasing in frequency, with the Polisario movement's number two, Mustapha Bachir Sayed, and with Driss Basri, Morocco's powerful minister of interior. The impact and likely product of identification, which they were able to deduce, was the premise for talking on both sides. Their early response gave me courage to hope that something could be arranged. By July, I was ready to meet in Algiers with the foreign minister and the secretary-general of the Algerian foreign ministry, since the tacit concurrence of Algiers was crucial. My proposal was an encounter at which anything could be discussed, bar independence pure and simple and integration pure and simple. There was always a rectangular coffee table in front of me wherever our meetings took place and I deployed as illustration a chopping gesture a little to the left of the table, saying: "There's straightforward integration," and a similar gesture beyond the right end: "There's straightforward independence. The subject for discussion is anything on the table; it can approach one or other extreme but not include it."

The Frente Polisario was keen to talk—that had long been its ambition—but there were conditions. First and foremost, the leaders did not wish to confront other Sahrawis, most especially those who had once been on their side; they wanted intercourse with Moroccans who had the power of decision, and in Polisario eyes there were only two: King Hassan and his son, the crown prince. A UN or third-party presence was also highly desirable to bear witness. The Moroccans were less animated at the prospect of talks—in fact they took some persuading—but, possibly because they had evaluated the situation and made an informed guess as to the consequences, they were prepared to consider my proposal, on two immutable conditions. The first condition was that any meeting between the crown and the Polisario leadership should remain secret, absolutely secret; in no circumstances was it to be exploited by Polisario to imply a degree of recognition or for public relations. The second condition was that any encounter could not be construed as taking place under official UN auspices, since there was no mandate to that effect, though they would work with me in a "personal" capacity.

There evolved a precarious meeting of minds. As I shuttled between Rabat and Rabouni for discussions, which were normally one to one to guarantee discretion, I detected an incipient willingness on each side to accommodate the minimum requirements of the other. On occasion I worried that too much depended on the word of one man and my interpretation of what he had said, and there were moments when we stumbled, but by early August 1996 the principle of an exploratory encounter was agreed. Over a weekend in Geneva, Basri met Bachir and they talked and lunched together, and as both of them told me afterward, each found the other worthy of further dialogue. The meeting, which had almost failed to happen for logistical reasons, exceeded expectations and provided good groundwork for a high-level encounter in Rabat. Polisario imposed several specific conditions; one was a wish not to be marooned "for security reasons" in an isolated villa. The delegates were accordingly offered accommodation at Rabat's premier hotel, and no restrictions were placed on their movements. There was a late hitch concerning air transport. The Frente Polisario did not consider it acceptable to arrive by a Moroccan aircraft of the king's flight, and Morocco was reluctant to have an official Algerian plane land at Rabat, where it would attract notice. At the last minute it was agreed to admit the Algerian flight, but to have it fly in at Tangier. The Polisario honored its commitment to secrecy and arrived discreetly with an impressive five-member delegation, well balanced tribally and drawn from the highest-ranking individuals, short of Abdel-Aziz, in its political and military life.

The crown prince of Morocco, advised by Basri, spent one and a half hours with the Polisario delegation during the evening after they arrived. Both characterized the atmosphere as very good. The following day saw some controversy, but an audience with the king was still envisaged. At the third session the word *independence* crept in (Bachir had a catchphrase about "independence with interdependence" that was clearly susceptible to varied interpretations), and the Moroccan side argued that the expected meeting with the king could not take place so long as Moroccan sovereignty was not recognized prior to the consideration of any proposals. The process may have moved too well too fast for certain vested interests, personal and political, and the conjecture is that pressure was applied. How sincere the two sides really were, how prepared to make the serious concessions they had hitherto refused, is hard to tell, but both reiterated their wish to pursue constructive dialogue and discussed tentative dates for a resumed meeting in the very near future. Relations remained positive as talking continued till the last minute, and the Frente Polisario delegation departed from Rabat on an aircraft of the king's flight.

The Polisario insisted that the next meeting be held outside Morocco, at a neutral venue; the Moroccans said that further dialogue involving the crown prince could take place only in Morocco. The Polisario really wanted a UN presence, or the presence of a friendly power, during talks; this Morocco rejected as irrelevant and inappropriate to a gathering of "Moroccans." These were small differences to overcome, given what U.S. influence readily imposed the following year.

For a brief moment this opening looked to be among the more promising in the history of MINURSO. The prospects for negotiation were enhanced by the successful identification of over 60,000 people, covering the great majority of those in the census, since both sides were in a position to estimate the number of qualified voters and reach an informed guess as to the future. The lack of absolute certainty was of benefit to talks. So was the likelihood that further identification, if indeed it could be made to happen, would only harden positions without leading to resolution, for by then the control that the shaikhs exercised through their power of rejection was obvious. The misfortune is that the opening occurred during the very months when great political events were evolving in the United States, events that of themselves had no bearing on Western Sahara but that came to play a direct role. Boutros-Ghali's term of office as UN Secretary-General was due to expire at the end of the year, and he sought a second mandate. President Bill Clinton also faced an election that year, and his ambassador at the UN, U.S. permanent representative Madeleine Albright, believed that U.S. interests were best served by ensuring that Boutros-Ghali be replaced. Bob Dole's Republican challenge to Clinton played on a widespread misrepresentation of the Secretary-General as commander in chief of UN forces including U.S. personnel, which was popularly rejected by Dole with a mocking parody of the name, "Boootros Boootros-Ghali." Boutros-Ghali alleged that the campaign to oust him was triggered by Albright's ambition to become secretary of state, something she denies although conceding that "near the end" the "two issues got tangled."[3] In these political circumstances the United States was not about to bolster the UN, and Boutros-Ghali himself became fixated on his reelection. Then Morocco and the Frente Polisario, once they had wind of possible change in the UN leadership, preferred to await the selection of a new Secretary-General, as both expressed it, "more favorable to their cause." It served to postpone the day of reckoning. The moment was lost.

During the General Assembly Fourth (Special Political and Decolonization) Committee debate on 10 October 1996, mention was made of the contacts' having taken place—by then they were no longer a secret; King Hassan himself referred to them in a public speech—but Morocco requested that the Secretary-General's report to the Security Council make no detailed reference to them.[4] The meetings, it was argued, were outside the framework of the settlement plan. In consequence, Boutros-Ghali's last Western Sahara report to the Council, on 5 November 1996, included nothing under his observations about the incipient dialogue or the hopes that it inspired. He focused on the reductions in MINURSO personnel—military, civil police, and civilian—and the major cost savings achieved. The Secretary-General yet again urged "the parties to continue cooperating . . . to find a resolution to the outstanding questions concerning the implementation of the settlement plan," and he bowed out.[5]

Kofi Annan became UN Secretary-General in January 1997. In his inaugural report to the Council on Western Sahara, he concluded a review of the situation with three questions: "(a) Can the settlement plan be implemented in its present form? (b) If not, are there adjustments to the settlement plan, acceptable to both parties, which would make it implementable? (c) If not, are there other ways by which the international community could help the parties resolve their conflict?" He went on to say: "The United Nations cannot compel the parties to honour their commitment to cooperate in implementing the settlement plan. Without such cooperation, it will become increasingly difficult to justify continuing expenditure."[6]

Although Kofi Annan had been undersecretary general for peacekeeping operations, he had not been personally engaged in the problems of Western Sahara. In my official briefing of him I described the achievement to date, the recent contacts with important compromises made on both sides, and what needed doing to move the process forward. In my view only the United States had sufficient interest in the region and the political weight and might be willing to play a role. France did not wish to become actively involved unless specifically requested by Morocco, as President Jacques Chirac had intimated to Boutros-Ghali. Were the United States to be directly engaged, there would be less carping about costs. Others may have given similar advice. In February the UN undersecretary general for political affairs was dispatched to Houston to sound out former U.S. secretary of state James A. Baker III and if possible persuade him "to accept an appointment as Special Representative and try to negotiate a deal based on enhanced autonomy for Western Sahara within the Kingdom of Morocco."[7]

Baker said that the time he had available was limited, but he accepted an appointment as the Secretary-General's personal envoy. The Secretary-General formally requested him "to assess the implementability of the plan, to examine ways of improving the chances of resuming its implementation in the near future and, if there were none, to advise me on other possible ways of moving the peace process forward."[8]

In the words of John Bolton, former U.S. assistant secretary of state for international organization affairs,

I think that the Secretary General approached Jim Baker for a couple of reasons, which were both wise and politically prudent from the UN's point of view. I think he recognized . . . that only an American was going to resolve this situation, if it could be resolved. . . .

I think the Secretary General also saw the two possibilities the Baker mission would have: number one, that it would succeed and bring about a free and fair referendum in the Western Sahara, that could be fairly described as a victory for the UN. . . . I think he wanted that. And I think he was hoping that Jim Baker could bring it home for him.

The other possibility, of course, was if the Baker mission failed, in which case, I believe, the Secretary General was prepared, and certainly Baker would have recommended, that MINURSO be terminated and the United Nations involvement cease. So that the Secretary General could then say, "We're not in these peace-keeping operations for infinity. We're going to try and take a shot and, if we don't get agreement by the parties, we're going to give it up," showing the Secretary General was a hard and decisive manager.[9]

James Baker's initial briefing took place in New York. I was advised by many not to delve too deeply into Sahrawi tribal lore. But if "all those subfractions and contested H41 and H61 and Chorfa and . . ." were so sure to confuse and bore him, he would not comprehend the rudiments of the problem and never understand why the settlement plan was stymied. I told him why. He sensed immediately that this was the core and that he needed to know the nettle before grasping it firmly. He posed supplementary questions. I explained that identification was stuck, and with it the prospect of establishing a convincing electoral roll. It would never be resolved to the satisfaction of both sides because the Polisario insisted and would always insist on jus soli with an electoral roll based principally on the 1974 Spanish census, while Morocco was equally insistent on jus sanguinis and an electoral roll comprising all Saharans with ties to the territory, very many of whom had not been included in the census for multiple reasons.

Baker wanted to know how identification worked. I told him that applicants included in the 1974 Spanish census had only to establish their personal identity, with pre-1975 documents rarely open to challenge, whereas other applicants relied on documentation issued by a party to the dispute, which was readily contested, and therefore depended on oral testimony to substantiate their claim. However, oral testimony posed a problem. The identification procedure provided for one shaikh of the subfraction from each side to confirm the applicant's personal identity and Sahrawi tribal affiliation. Whatever our original assumptions about abstention might have been, a political pattern was quick to emerge. In dubious cases—and most cases relying on oral testimony were to an extent dubious—the Polisario shaikh could cast a negative vote, which effectively vetoed whatever the shaikh from the Moroccan side might say. The "Moroccan" shaikhs could not cancel that out by blocking potential voters from the other side, since these benefited from inclusion in the revised list. It might, just might, be possible to jump-start identification again, but any resumption of identification would lead eventually to the same dead end: an outcome one or the other would be bound to contest.

It was my assessment, and that of many well-informed observers, that a referendum on a politically negotiated deal, presumably involving a fair degree of autonomy for Western Sahara within the Kingdom of Morocco, offered the most realistic way of permitting self-determination. The winner-take-all conclusion of the settlement plan militated against any compromise in implementation. King Hassan had himself adopted the phrase *ni vainqueur, ni vaincu*—"neither conqueror, nor conquered"—as the formula to be preferred. Finally, it was worth bearing in mind that the settlement plan was based on the parties' cooperating; there were no threats to ensure compliance, and no mechanism was envisaged to impose whatever solution might be arrived at.

It was not everyone's view at the time. Bolton, who attended the briefing in New York, commented later:

> When Secretary Baker was preparing to go out to the region for the first time, he was advised by virtually every expert (and people who weren't necessarily experts but had opinions on the subject) that the referendum process could never work. It could never work. It was a bad idea. They believed that the idea of an either-or choice between independence for the Western Sahara or amalgamation with Morocco was the kind of choice that didn't permit a negotiated resolution, and that neither side would ever really agree to what they already agreed to several times before.
>
> But to their surprise, and I think to everyone's surprise, when Secretary Baker went to the region and asked the King, asked the government of Morocco, asked the leadership of the Polisario, "What do you want?" they said, without hesitation and without equivocation, "We want a free and fair referendum." "Want to talk about autonomy?" "No, we don't want to talk about autonomy. We want to talk about a referendum."[10]

Baker visited the region from 23 to 28 April 1997. In Rabat he was received by King Hassan and had meetings with the top Moroccan establishment; in Tindouf he met with the secretary-general of the Frente Polisario, Mohamed Abdel-Aziz, and others of the Polisario leadership; in Algiers and in Mauritania he was received by both presidents and talked to ministers and officials. I was with Baker as his adviser except for two crucial tête-à-tête encounters with Hassan and Abdel-Aziz. Baker also had as aides two distinguished Americans: Chester A. Crocker, former U.S. assistant secretary of state for African affairs, and John R. Bolton. Both had served under him in the State Department.

Baker is an astute and highly experienced politician, a statesman of stature who selects his advisers, listens attentively to the counsel they give, asks probing questions, and arrives at his own judgment. He was given, in the strictest confidence, not only all the facts and figures pertaining to identification but the scrupulously calculated projections that we had prepared. I had used some of the same elements to convince Morocco and the Polisario to meet the previous year, though I gave them no precise numbers and nothing in writing. The projections indicated that the established identification procedure, and it was hard to envisage the parties accepting any other—indeed they had fiercely rejected the variants suggested earlier—would never escape political manipulation. Oral testimony would not be allowed to prevail, and the roll of eligible voters would end by reflecting the 1974 census plus a modest percentage. Morocco was bound to reject an outcome that so categorically discriminated against the tens of thousands who had been encouraged to apply, leaving a potential electorate of dubious loyalty to its cause, while Polisario would be spurred on to demand the referendum and nothing less than the option of independence.

Whether Baker presented these arguments, with supporting data, to King Hassan is unclear; they talked privately (through an interpreter) as they strolled in the evening air. But as we drove away from the palace, Baker informed me that the king chose to move ahead with the settlement plan; perhaps he wished to buy time. That Polisario wanted the plan was less surprising. To restore the plan to life, Baker told the parties, direct talks were necessary.

During the months afterward, brief, intensive, and tough negotiations took place. The first session, in London, was to agree to meet face to face. Three weekend rounds followed, in Lisbon, London, and Lisbon again, before the concluding conference at the Baker Institute for Public Policy at Rice University in Houston, Texas, from 14 to 16 September. Baker proved a consummate negotiator, and above all he was an American, with the proverbial big stick always present in everyone's mental background. As Bolton was to say, "I think only an American could have filled the role that Baker did."[11] Morocco liked to stress the continuing importance of its U.S. alliance; Polisario espoused U.S. anti-imperialist sentiments and commitment to the self-determination ideal and, equally important, believed that the United States had the clout to move Morocco.

Baker's negotiating principles were made explicit at the outset. As personal envoy of the Secretary-General, he would make suggestions and offer ideas; but he would have no power to impose solutions or veto agreements; there was to be complete confidentiality; and "no issue would be considered final until all outstanding issues were agreed."[12] On 24 September the Secretary-General reported the results to the Security Council.[13] In annexes to his report he set out the compromises reached on outstanding identification issues, outstanding refugee issues, troop confinement, prisoners of war, and political prisoners and detainees. A third annex opened with a "declaration of the parties," provided a code of conduct for the referendum campaign in Western Sahara, and culminated with "practical measures to be taken for the resumption of identification."[14]

Identification was back in pole position. The compromise, which had been craftily articulated to balance something taken with something received, gave Morocco the right to have applicants from the contested groups H, I, and J identified, but at the same time Morocco was enjoined from sponsoring or presenting, directly or indirectly, anyone from H41, H61, and J51/52 not included in the 1974 census or their immediate family members; however, there was no obligation actively to prevent individuals from presenting themselves. Polisario was given satisfaction by the agreement that the Secretary-General's special representative would notify the parties of the results by number, though not by name, of the identification process to date. Morocco was assured that oral testimony would be received and considered by the Identification Commission. The Secretary-General concluded that upon completion of the last round, all that had been agreed in London, Lisbon, and Houston would take effect. These achievements, he maintained, created "the conditions to proceed towards full implementation of the settlement plan, starting with the resumption of the identification process."[15]

Some of us were less convinced. There was speculation as to the number of persons from the contested groups who would come forward of their own volition, how Morocco would interpret the interdiction on "sponsoring," and whether Baker had been given any assurances in secret. The rocks likely to impede and endanger identification remained beneath the surface, only temporarily submerged by the Bakerine tide. There had been no change in the basic position of either Morocco or the Frente Polisario, positions that were destined to harden once the results of identification were confirmed officially. The Houston agreement obliged the parties to identify applicants presenting themselves from the H41, H61, and J51/52 census categories but failed to address the vexed issue of the selection of shaikhs for these groups or how oral testimony should be evaluated.

It was my opinion that a brief resumption of identification in which some from the contested were identified and the noncontested largely completed—which could have been accomplished crisply—would have rammed home to both sides the likely outcome without imposing a straitjacket. To force-feed a reluctant Polisario with the identification of the most contested would inevitably produce a result that Morocco would reject because it would depend on oral testimony, and by then we already knew the fate of evidence given orally before two shaikhs, or shaikh substitutes, drawn from opposing camps. It was disappointing for me to realize that an American as head of mission was deemed desirable to ensure continuing budgetary as well as political support in Washington. My disappointment at not being able to see the mission through to a successful conclusion was qualified by strong doubt that the Houston accord was destined to lead to self-determination by way of the settlement plan.

Since a new head of mission would be unfamiliar with the complexities and arcane nature of identification and, of course, unaware of the minefields and booby traps, the Secretary-General requested that I take responsibility for putting the show back on the road. Frenetic activity followed. Identification Commission members, language staff, data-processing polyglots, and support personnel had to be unearthed, recruited—through the UN's meticulous and sometimes cumbersome procedures—trained (since only a few of the original team were instantly reavailable), and deployed. Convocation lists were dispatched to the parties—the Polisario complained that the notice was slightly shorter than it should have been—centers were reopened, transport was organized, and other practical arrangements were completed by the deadline imposed so as to maintain "political momentum." The message from Baker had been that speed was essential. On 3 December 1997, identification resumed. Here was proof that the UN could act expeditiously when required.

At the operational level there were signs of improvement. For example, when Morocco asked that 900 individuals convoked at Tan-Tan be identified at Goulemine, and the Polisario was unwilling to accept any change, the commission ruled this to be a technical matter within its competence to resolve. But the agreement not to sponsor directly or indirectly anyone from H41, H61, or J51/52, other than those included in the 1974 census and their immediate family, was quick to come under strain. It had been agreed that we should begin by processing applicants from the three disputed groups: Morocco had long been anxious that they come forward for identification, and Polisario, I suspected, wanted to experience how Houston would translate into practice. The first batch of 830 applicants, all census listed, was duly convoked for identification in Laayoune. That day 3,927 unconvoked individuals presented themselves, and in the succeeding days a further 8,613 persons arrived at the center. It was already doubtful how the process would evolve; it was patently certain to take much longer than first envisaged. The Secretary-General expressed to the Security Council his doubts that the identification process could be concluded in time to permit the start of the transitional period on 7 June 1998 as planned.[16]

On 26 February 1998, I handed over responsibility as head of mission to U.S. diplomat Charles A. Dunbar, newly appointed as special representative of the Secretary-General. By then, in addition to the 77,058 convoked and 60,112 persons identified by the end of 1995, a further 45,705 had been convoked and 34,049 identified, bringing the grand total of those identified to 94,161. But I departed MINURSO with foreboding.

Identification staggered on. The pace was uneven. Rabat was reluctant to begin identification at two new centers in northern Morocco and to complete identifying certain unconvoked applicants, pending clarification of how other possible applicants from the three contested tribal groupings would be dealt with. There were interruptions arising from perceived slights and accusations. A new concern was the almost daily appearance in the Moroccan press of accusations of an alleged bias against Moroccan-sponsored applicants on the part of the UN Identification Commission.[17] While identification advanced reasonably smoothly for tribal groups other than H41, H61, and J51/52 and was even projected to finish by August, Morocco refused to take part in identifying applicants from those three groups listed in the census and their family members until the overall issue of identifying all applicants had been settled. Identification was also halted at the Zouerate center in Mauritania when Morocco contested the right of applicants previously resident in the camps at Tindouf to transfer their place of residence.

Finally, in his September 1998 report to the Security Council, the Secretary-General was able to confirm that all applicants from tribes other than the H41, H61, and J51/52 tribal groupings had been convoked and their identification could be regarded as complete, with only a few exceptions: those who came forward for identification in Mauritania after being registered in the Tindouf camps and several hundred persons resident abroad. But these "could use the appeals process in order to seek inclusion in the voters' list." A total of 147,350 individuals had been interviewed by the Identification Commission. Unfortunately, "no proposals have been forthcoming from either party that would permit the resumption of identification of applicants from tribal groupings H41, H51 [sic] and J51/52." The Secretary-General was concerned. He noted that his personal envoy was pursuing his contacts with the parties to assess whether the settlement plan could be carried out in its present form or whether there might be adjustments to it, acceptable to the parties, that would improve the chances of implementing it. "If he concludes that, even with adjustments, the Plan cannot be carried out, he will advise me on other courses of action that could be pursued."[18]

A package of measures was proposed to salvage the process. The key provisions were: the initiation of the appeals process for already identified applicants at the same time as the identification of remaining applicants from the tribal groupings H41, H61 and J51/52 wishing to present themselves individually; the effective formalization of the presence of the Office of the High Commissioner for Refugees in the territory to allow the necessary preparation for the repatriation of refugees and other Saharans residing outside the territory found eligible to vote together with their immediate families; and a revised schedule, under which the referendum would be held in December 1999.[19] The Frente Polisario formally accepted the package during Kofi Annan's visit to the region in late 1998; after expressing concerns and seeking clarification, Morocco communicated agreement in principle in March 1999. Consultations in Rabat and in New York led to revision of the texts and a revised timetable.

Dunbar resigned at the end of March 1999 after little more than a year in office. He had been hoping for movement on refugee repatriation—a worthy humanitarian objective but somewhat unlikely. Morocco always maintained that the people in the camps were "sequestered" and held there against their real interest, which was to return home to Western Sahara. Most, it is true, had family members with whom they wished to be reunited, but after twenty or more long years in the camps, bombarded by the inevitable propaganda that emanated from both sides, informed and objective freedom of opinion was in short supply. From a practical angle, personal travel beyond the camps was near impossible, but even with full liberty of movement (except for the leaders, liberty of movement outside the Tindouf area was circumscribed), the Polisario supporters were as likely to opt to endure until the referendum liberated them. What was more, Polisario's ambitions relied on refugee numbers and their continuing presence. A further complication emerged after Houston: to accommodate the settlement plan requirement that voting in the referendum as well as the preceding campaign occur in the territory, the Polisario demanded repatriation to the "liberated" zone east of the berm. That was politically out of the question for Morocco. Politically acceptable or not, from a realistic point of view it was hard to envisage tens of thousands of people and any livestock they might bring being accommodated in barren desert with no significant settlements and few water holes.

Finally, on 15 June 1999, identification resumed in accordance with meticulous proposals set out in a protocol and operational directives.[20] In respect of the numerous and most contentious H61, it was provided that both sides be free to nominate whomever they wished to perform the function of shaikh, on condition only that he had reached the age of eighteen by December 1993; he was allowed advisers to assist him. The "veto" problem was indirectly addressed: "Concordant testimony from the two sheikhs is not a *sine qua non* for eligibility. In the event of conflicting oral testimony from the two sheikhs, the Commission shall take a decision on eligibility in accordance with the provisions of paragraph 9 above."[21] According to that paragraph, "decisions on eligibility shall be taken at the centre where identification takes place, taking into account the relevance of all the evidence, both oral and written, and all available information, including the comments of the parties and the data regarding other members of the applicant's family."[22] It would be no easy task for members of the commission to overrule the word of a shaikh. The appeals process was scheduled to start mid-July, in tandem with the publication of the first part of the provisional voters list. The Secretary-General urged the parties to "stay the course."[23]

Once again the process was restarted on terms differently interpreted by the two sides and with no prospect that both would find the end product palatable.

Identification of applicants, scrupulously referred to in the reports as "individual applicants," from tribal groupings H41, H61, and J51/52 proceeded and was expected to finish by the end of the year. This was achieved, just on schedule, on 30 December 1999.[24] The Secretary-General was constrained to report, however, that a "relatively small percentage of applicants from the . . . three tribal groupings has been found eligible by the Identification Commission." In consequence, he concluded, "if all those who may be found ineligible were to file an appeal, the total number of appeals to be processed could almost double." Some 79,000 appeals had already been filed when the first part of the voters' list was published in July. Appeals were filed by "almost all the applicants who, on the basis of their interviews, did not meet the criteria for voter eligibility."[25] Most appeals indicated the names of witnesses who would provide new facts to support a claim for inclusion. The Frente Polisario, referring to the section on appeals submitted with the protocol and operational directives relating to identification, hotly contested the admissibility of large numbers of appeals.[26] Morocco invoked the Security Council resolution reaffirming the rights of applicants, that every prospective voter had the right of appeal and that "admissibility requirements could be fulfilled by the naming of witnesses who would provide new information."[27] The Identification Commission was stymied. The Secretary-General despaired of holding a referendum "before 2002 or even beyond."[28]

On 17 January 2000, the second part of the provisional voter list was released. Of the 51,220 persons interviewed from tribal groupings H41, H61, and J51/52, only 2,135 had been found eligible to vote. The reaction was predictable. The Moroccan authorities "expressed surprise and dismay" and stressed the importance of the appeals process "in which all Saharans rejected by the MINURSO Identification Commission are given the opportunity to restate their case." Moroccan officials went on to question again "the impartiality and objectivity of Identification Commission members and warned that the referendum would not be held if any person originating from the Sahara were denied the right to participate."[29] The Frente Polisario, on the other hand, admonished against any attempt to delay the referendum and added ominously that if the process was deferred much longer there could be a return to hostilities.

By the time identification eventually finished, a grand total of 195,589 individuals had been interviewed. The final figure for those found eligible to vote came to 86,412—a moderate percentage increment to the 72,370 on the revised 1974 census list. Appeals, against inclusion (anyone found eligible had the right to object to other names) as well as omission, ultimately reached 131,038.[30] The prospect of repeating much of the process, relying on the oral testimony of witnesses, before the shaikhs and in the presence of embittered party representatives, was not merely daunting, it was unrealistic.

In his report to the Security Council in February 2000, the Secretary-General provided a historical overview of the mission's achievements and how identification, after its launch in August 1994, had proceeded in spite of constant difficulties and in the face of the parties' divergent interpretations. The appointment of James Baker as personal envoy had produced the Houston accords, paving the way for the resumption of identification, only to run into many of the same obstacles encountered earlier. In the end the inevitable conclusion was that of the fundamental differences between the parties over the interpretation of the settlement plan, "the issue of the establishment of the electorate has been, and may remain, a core problem which could eventually prevent the holding of a referendum as provided by the plan." The difficulties and delays encountered in identification had made it all too apparent that Morocco and the Frente Polisario were both convinced that "the composition of the electoral body will predetermine the outcome of the referendum." There could be little doubt that the same concerns would permeate any appeals process. The parties had conflicting views on admissibility. Were a compromise formula reached to overcome that obstacle, the prospect of tens of thousands of appeals in addition to those already received ruled out a realistic timetable. And that was not the only problem: the repatriation of refugees, appropriate security measures, and more remained contentious. Finally, the Secretary-General highlighted an inescapable fact that had rarely been made explicit: "Even assuming that a referendum were held pursuant to the settlement plan and agreements of the parties, if the result were not to be recognized and accepted by one party, it is worth noting that no enforcement mechanism is envisaged by the settlement plan, nor is one likely to be proposed, calling for the use of military means to effect enforcement."[31]

Notes

1. Report of the Secretary-General, S/1996/343 (8 May 1996), pars. 30 seq., 35, 36.
2. Security Council Resolution 1056(1996), 29 May 1996.
3. Madeleine Albright, *Madam Secretary* (London: Macmillan, 2003), 212n1.
4. See Report of the Secretary-General, S/1996/913 (5 November 1996), par. 5.
5. Ibid., par. 29.
6. Report of the Secretary-General, S/1997/166 (27 February 1997), pars. 17, 19.
7. Marrack Goulding, *Peacemonger* (London: John Murray, 2002), 214.
8. Report of the Secretary-General, S/1997/358 (5 May 1997), par. 3.
9. John Bolton, "Resolving the Western Sahara Conflict," transcript of the Congressional Defense and Foreign Policy Forum, Washington, D.C., 1998, 5–6.

10. Ibid., 6–7.

11. Ibid., 7, par. 3.

12. Report of the Secretary-General, S/1997/742 of 24 September 1997, par. 6.

13. Ibid.

14. Ibid., Annexes I, II, III.

15. Ibid., par. 27.

16. Report of the Secretary-General, S/1998/35 (15 January 1998), par. 31.

17. Report of the Secretary-General, S/1998/316 (13 April 1998), par. 6.

18. Report of the Secretary-General, S/1998/849 (11 September 1998), pars. 2–4, 23.

19. Report of the Secretary-General, S/1999/307 of 22 March 1999, par. 2.

20. Report of the Secretary-General. S/1999/483 (13 May 1999), Addendum I.

21. Ibid., under III, "Special Rules Concerning the Manner of Conducting the Identification," par. 12 (iv).

22. Ibid., "Identification Operations," par. 9.

23. Report of the Secretary-General, S/1999/721 (25 June 1999), par. 15.

24. Report of the Secretary-General, S/2000/131 (17 February 2000), par. 6.

25. Report of the Secretary-General, S/1999/1219 (6 December 1999), pars. 8–9.

26. Report of the Secretary-General, S/1999/483 (13 May 1999), Addendum I, 13–14.

27. Security Council Resolution 1263(1999), 13 September 1999.

28. Report of the Secretary-General, S/1999/1219 (6 December 1999), par. 28.

29. Report of the Secretary-General, S/2000/131 (17 February 2000), par. 5.

30. Report of the Secretary-General, S/2001/148 (20 February 2001), Annex I, repeated in Report of the Secretary-General, S/2002/178 (19 February 2002), par. 26.

31. Report of the Secretary-General, S/2000/131 (17 February 2000), pars. 32–33, 36.

8

Searching for Alternatives

James Baker was invited to make a renewed effort to explore ways and means to achieve an early, durable, and agreed resolution of the dispute. At a meeting in London on 14 May 2000, the first time that the parties had come face to face since the talks in 1997, the views expressed served only to reaffirm the widely divergent positions, and no constructive suggestions emerged that might move the process ahead. A second London meeting, on 28 June, gave Morocco and the Frente Polisario the opportunity to make their case and offer proposals. There was no progress. According to Baker, "Neither party had shown any disposition to depart from the 'winner-take-all' mentality or appeared willing to discuss any possible political solutions in which each would get some, but not all, of what it wanted and would allow the other side to do the same." After asking the parties for concrete proposals and receiving none, he decided that "the meeting, instead of resolving problems, had in fact moved things backwards as it had deepened the differences between the parties."[1]

Reporting to the Security Council on the failed meeting, the Secretary-General quoted Baker on the nature of a political solution. It could be "a negotiated agreement for full integration with Morocco; a negotiated agreement for full independence; a negotiated agreement for something in between; or a negotiated agreement that would permit a successful implementation of the settlement plan." However, it had to be repeated that "the positions of the parties in interpreting some of the key provisions of the settlement plan, and the problems encountered over the past nine years to achieve its implementation, do not augur well for that prospect." The Secretary-General concurred that "arriving at a political solution is far more preferable than a breakdown of the process which might lead to a return to hostilities, something that must be avoided at all costs."[2]

*   *   *

Technical meetings at the expert level took place in Geneva on 21–22 July. They were equally nonproductive. Subsequent discussions with each party concentrated on prisoners of war, presumed political detainees, and steps to implement confidence-building measures. The only positive development was Morocco's "accounting of the status of the 207 presumed political detainees." The attempt to start consideration of appeals fell before the first fence: "the Moroccan delegation stated it was not authorized to discuss the appeals process, because the problems regarding that issue were political and not technical."[3]

A meeting in Berlin on 28 September 2000 with the personal envoy himself fared little better. Although Morocco and the Frente Polisario both continued intoning their commitment to the settlement plan, there was no change in their positions. Baker was forced to conclude that "there was no political will on either side." He sketched the alternative scenarios: self-determination through war or revolution, through elections, which required the necessary good will, or through agreement. Polisario reacted by reiterating commitment to the settlement plan and their readiness to discuss the appeals process. Morocco stated categorically that the way "the plan was being implemented meant that two-thirds of the Saharan population would be excluded from the referendum."[4] When Baker suggested, true to his balanced negotiating technique, that the parties explore ways to move the appeals process forward while at the same time searching for a political solution, Morocco reacted by saying that the appeals question had been exhaustively covered and was deadlocked not on technicalities but on position; Polisario said it was not ready to discuss anything outside the settlement plan.

Reporting to the Council, the Secretary-General reverted to his personal envoy's original mandate to assess the implementability of the settlement plan, to examine whether adjustments acceptable to the parties would improve chances for its implementation, and, failing that, to recommend other ways of resolving the conflict. He had come to the conclusion that "further meetings of the parties to seek a political solution cannot succeed . . . unless the Government of Morocco as administrative Power in Western Sahara is prepared to offer or support some devolution of governmental authority, for all the inhabitants and former inhabitants of the Territory, that is genuine, substantial and in keeping with international norms."[5]

Tension between the two sides was exacerbated when the Paris-Dakar motor rally was announced as passing through Western Sahara. It was not the first time; it had happened previously, most recently in 1999, but on this occasion the organizers had consulted only Morocco. The Frente Polisario, profoundly frustrated at the deadlocked settlement plan, reacted vehemently:

passage of the rally would be in violation of the cease-fire, and the Polis-ario would resume military action, in self-defense, on the day the rally entered the territory.[6] As it happened, when, on 7 January 2001, the rally crossed into Western Sahara, the Frente Polisario issued a brief commu-niqué affirming that the crossing constituted a flagrant breach of the cease-fire, for which they held Morocco responsible, but adding that following appeals from the OAU chairman, friendly countries (including Algeria), and the United States, they had decided to suspend the decision to resume military activities.[7] However, Polisario units were deployed outside their confinement locations without prior notification, and restrictions were imposed on MINURSO military observers' freedom of movement for air and ground patrols—contravening cease-fire agreements. Polisario accused a Moroccan army unit of having penetrated the buffer zone.[8]

There was no progress on appeals or any aspect of the settlement plan, nor was there clear indication that Morocco would be prepared to offer devolution of authority as outlined by Baker. The only positive develop-ment was the Frente Polisario release, on humanitarian grounds, of 201 Moroccan prisoners of war.[9]

In late spring, James Baker renewed in earnest the effort to determine whether Morocco might be willing to devolve authority that would be "gen-uine, substantial and in keeping with international norms." Morocco's reac-tion was to restate commitment to the settlement plan while recalling the many obstacles, which were not merely technical: "There were errors and distortions in the implementation of the plan, which could not satisfy the thousands of rejected applicants. . . . The way it was being implemented meant that two-thirds of the Saharan population would be excluded from the referendum." Morocco lamented that "despite all good will, the diffi-culties faced in the implementation of the plan could not be overcome." Yet wishing "to further explore other ways and means to settle the conflict, . . . Morroco was prepared to initiate a sincere and frank dialogue with the other party on the dispute that had divided them for almost 25 years." The Frente Polisario, for its part, reiterated that "it would cooperate and adhere to any dialogue that would be within the framework of the settlement plan since, in its view, other solutions had been overtaken by events."[10]

The Polisario was determined not to let go of the bone that was theirs at last: an identification process that had produced what they had always wanted, an electoral roll only modestly inflated from the 1974 census and pointing straight at the referendum to which they aspired. The changing demography of Western Sahara made any regional autonomy alternative far less attractive to them than in the past. In Morocco, however, the plan was pronounced dead, and there could be no merit in trying to resurrect a process from which, as they insisted, "two-thirds of the Saharan population would be excluded." The Moroccans also knew that Western Sahara was no longer the place it had been in 1975 and that its demography continued to change.

The Secretary-General fully agreed with his personal envoy that the time might have come to move beyond the plan, given the "serious doubts as to whether the settlement plan can be implemented in its present form in a way that will result in an early, durable and agreed resolution of the dispute over Western Sahara."[11] Annexed to his report to the Security Council on 20 June 2001 was a "Framework Agreement on the Status of Western Sahara," devised by Baker. It was described as "not unlike agreements used to address similar situations elsewhere where a devolution of authority to the inhabitants of a non-self-governing territory is granted with the final status of the territory to be determined by a referendum."[12] The draft framework agreement conferred on the "population" of Western Sahara the right to elect their own executive and legislative bodies and to have exclusive competence over local government administration, territorial budget and taxation, law enforcement, internal security, social welfare, culture, education, commerce, transportation, agriculture, mining, fisheries and industry, environmental policy, housing and urban development, water and electricity, roads, and other basic infrastructure. Morocco would have exclusive competence over foreign relations, national security (including antisecession measures), and external defense, and the flag, currency, customs, and postal and communications systems of the Morrocan kingdom should be the same for Western Sahara. The criteria for election of the executive, based on the eligible voters' list, favored Polisario, but all persons aged eighteen or over who had been continuously resident since 31 October 1998 or were included in the repatriation list would have the right to participate in the referendum on the final status of the territory.

Morocco, reluctant though it professed to be, was prepared to treat the proposal seriously.[13] The Frente Polisario, in a barely controlled explosion, expressed total opposition to any solution ignoring its inalienable right to self-determination and provided proposals to overcome obstacles and move the settlement plan on toward the referendum.[14] Algeria added its voice in support of Polisario.[15]

That August, Baker invited Polisario, Algeria, and (basically as an observer) Mauritania to his ranch at Pinedale, Wyoming, to clarify aspects of the proposed framework agreement, but neither Polisario nor Algeria was willing to engage in detailed discussion of the draft. Subsequently, the Polisario provided Baker with detailed clarifications of why the draft framework agreement did not offer a basis for settling the Western Sahara problem or even a means of relaunching negotiations: what it did was pave the way for "the precipitous integration of the Saharan Territory into Morocco." In the view of the Frente Polisario,

By conferring on Morocco exclusive competence over "the preservation of the territorial integrity against secessionist attempts whether from within or without the territory" and by allowing it to maintain its troops, police, administration and authority in the Territory, the proposed framework agreement in effect grants Morocco the attributes of sovereignty, especially since, in the words of the draft, "all laws . . . and all decisions of the courts must respect and comply with the constitution of the Kingdom of Morocco."[16]

Polisario then contributed specific proposals for reviving the settlement plan, which, in contrast to the framework agreement, offered the Saharan people a free, fair and impartial referendum and thus the prospect of exercising their inalienable right to self-determination. Algeria also submitted a lengthy, detailed, and critical analysis of the draft and proposed instead that the UN assume sovereignty over Western Sahara in order to implement provisions largely identical to the settlement plan.[17]

The observations of the Frente Polisario and Algeria were forwarded to the government of Morocco on 31 October.[18] The response came quickly: on 10 November, Morocco dismissed the attempt to resurrect pursuit of the settlement plan when "all such efforts have clearly ended in deadlock." It focused on the draft framework agreement. In a strong defense of the legality of its presence and its administration in Western Sahara, it cited the Madrid Agreement of 1975 and argued that Morocco had "recovered its provinces of 'Western Sahara' in the same way that it had recovered the neighbouring provinces of Tarfaya and Sidi Ifni following negotiations with Spain, in 1958 and in 1969." Problems arose only because "the settlement of the question of the Sahara in accordance with international law did not suit Algeria, which deliberately chose to create a regional dispute, in a totally artificial way, and has taken steps to internationalise it."[19]

During January 2002, the personal envoy visited Morocco and was received twice by King Mohammed VI (King Hassan had died the previous year), met President Abdelaziz Bouteflika in Algiers, and met Mohamed Abdel-Aziz, secretary-general of the Frente Polisario, near Tindouf. All Baker could say afterward was that there was not any "real chance that the parties will ultimately voluntarily agree to this approach to solve their dispute over Western Sahara" and it was, therefore, pointless "to pursue . . . any more discussion on the draft framework agreement, as neither the Government of Algeria nor the Frente Polisario is willing to engage in discussing it."[20] Reporting that assessment to the Council, the Secretary-General agreed with Baker: it was "highly unlikely that the settlement plan can be implemented in its present form in a way that it will achieve an early durable and agreed resolution of the dispute over Western Sahara."[21] In these bleak circumstances, Kofi Annan took an unusual step. He presented the Council with four options from which to select one—not a compromise yoking of two—for Baker to develop a "solution," which the Council would then impose on the parties in a radical departure from the nonbinding exercise of good offices.

The first option would be to resume implementation of the settlement plan but without requiring the concurrence of both parties. This was a daunting prospect: the effort was likely to take years without any guarantee that the UN could conduct a free and fair referendum whose results would be accepted by both sides, and there would be no mechanism to enforce the results. As a second option, the personal envoy would revise the draft framework agreement, taking into account the concerns expressed, but without seeking the concurrence of the parties. "The revised framework agreement would be submitted to the Security Council, and the Council would then present it to the parties on a non-negotiable basis." Option three would have the Council ask the personal envoy to explore with the parties a possible division of the territory. Once again, were the parties unable to agree upon a division by 1 November 2002, the personal envoy would be asked to submit to the Security Council a proposal for dividing the territory, and the Council would present this to the parties on a nonnegotiable basis. As a fourth option, the Council could decide to terminate MINURSO, "thereby recognizing and acknowledging that after more than 11 years and the expenditure of sums of money nearing half a billion dollars, the United Nations is not going to solve the problem of Western Sahara without requiring that one or the other or both of the parties do something that they do not wish to voluntarily agree to do."[22]

Option one was unrealistic, and the Council was unwilling to end MINURSO. That left options two and three. James Baker had addressed members during informal consultations and he was thought to have shown a preference for a revised framework agreement; he replied to a question that he already had certain ideas about amendments. The idea of dividing the territory was attributed to a conversation Baker had had with Bouteflika of Algeria, but this held little appeal even for Polisario (who may have remembered the 1979 peace agreement following the change of regime in Mauritania); Baker had not yet studied it further. An even bigger problem was the suggestion that the Council move beyond a settlement based on consensus to an imposed solution.

The Council was in a quandary. It chose to extend MINURSO's mandate for two months while it considered the options "actively."[23] Two months later the Secretary-General confirmed that his personal envoy "stands ready to undertake the activities that will be required under the option [singular] that the Security Council chooses . . . provided that the Council does not support any changes to option one, two or three that would require the concurrence of the parties. Such changes . . . would simply encourage a continuation of the conflict and the current stalemate."[24] Still the Council demurred: more time was needed.

Another three months passed, and the clear, strong mandate that Baker wanted remained elusive. The idea had been for Council "experts" to consider one option per month, but the diametrically opposed party positions, bolstered by arcane argument, resisted compression into tidy boxes, and Council members were divided in their political sympathies. Informal consultations during July 2000 proved exceptionally tense for Western Sahara. The United Kingdom, as president for the month, began early consideration of a draft resolution in support of Baker's preference, put forward by the United States with backing from France. Although the United States was reported to be working hard to muster support also in capitals, the draft resolution did not gain general acceptance. Russia, with considerable support from nonpermanent members, argued for a two-track approach. The United States, France, and the UK supported Baker's desire for a clear mandate and saw the dual option as a prescription for further prevarication. It was rumored that Baker would resign if not given his precise, compelling mandate. It was even whispered that the United States could veto the extension of MINURSO's mandate if the Council refused to comply: of all the Council members, only the United States seemed willing to contemplate closing the mission. Russia stayed firm as the United States worked for a simple majority vote—which would be a departure from MINURSO's tradition of consensus, but even a majority could not be taken for granted. Several members refused to jettison, as they saw it, the basic principle of self-determination, and there was opposition to a nonconsensual approach, with the exercise of good offices being transformed into binding arbitration.

From the sidelines, Morocco undertook to be genuinely flexible about the framework agreement. Algeria reiterated its preference for the settlement plan—which was impeded only by a lack of political will—but, failing that, expressed a willingness to explore partition of the territory. The United States tabled a modified draft of the resolution in support of a revised framework agreement, now including the phrase "which provides for self-determination," to be submitted to the Council, reviewed, and then presented to the parties. Algeria and the Frente Polisario both addressed themselves to the Council president, rejecting this approach roundly.

Efforts to achieve a compromise proved impossible. The president concluded that the options had in effect become a "prison," and he proposed a technical roll-over, a six-month extension of the mandate. During this period the personal envoy would pursue dialogue not tied to any specific option; the Council president confirmed that Baker was willing to continue. The resolution, as adopted after amendment, went beyond a simple roll-over. It gave Baker six months to propose a political solution, presumably other than the alternatives suggested earlier, bearing in mind the parties' concerns and providing for self-determination. There was no hint that this would then be imposed on the parties with or without their consent, and certainly there was no mention of machinery for enforcement.[25]

On 5 November 2002, in his speech to the nation on the occasion of the twenty-seventh anniversary of the Green March, King Mohammed VI of Morocco declared that there was increasing support in the international community for a political solution and this in the context of respect for the sovereignty and territorial integrity of Morocco. Such a solution would render the referendum envisaged in the UN settlement plan "lapsed because not applicable"—*Caduc, car inapplicable.*[26]

In January 2003, Baker went to the region and confidentially presented some new ideas to Morocco and the Frente Polisario; they were given two months to respond. The Council obliged by extending MINURSO's mandate accordingly. By the time the comments were received in mid-March, the Security Council was in the throes of its own war over Iraq; Western Sahara was again deferred. Two months later, the Secretary-General presented to the Security Council, in annex to his analysis of the process to date, Baker's "Peace Plan for Self-Determination of the People of Western Sahara."[27] Also annexed were the responses of Morocco, the Frente Polisario, and the neighboring states Algeria and Mauritania.[28] Calling it the "peace plan" caused some confusion in the region, where the original "settlement plan" was commonly known as the *plan de paix,* but the Baker plan was different. It went beyond the "framework agreement" to spell out in some detail provisions for a referendum of self-determination to be held no earlier than four and no later than five years after the effective date of the plan's implementation. Those eligible to vote would be all persons aged eighteen or over included in MINURSO's provisional voter list (without giving effect to any appeals or other objections); those whose names appeared on the repatriation list drawn up by UNHCR as of 31 October 2000; and those who had resided continually in Western Sahara since 30 December 1999. Eligibility would be determined by the UN, whose decision "shall be final and without appeal."[29]

Until such time as the new government took office, governmental authority would be vested in executive, legislative, and judicial bodies collectively referred to as the Western Sahara Authority. The Authority would be responsible for, and have exclusive competence over, local government, the territorial budget, taxation, economic development, internal security, law enforcement, social welfare, cultural affairs, education, commerce, transportation, agriculture, mining, fisheries, industry, environment, housing and urban development, water and electricity, roads, and other basic infrastructure. Morocco would have exclusive competence over foreign relations, national security and external defense, matters relating to weapons and the preservation of territorial integrity against secessionist attempts; in addition, the flag, currency, customs, and postal and telecommunication systems of Morocco should be the same for Western Sahara. Legislative authority was to be exercised by a legislative assembly, which would be responsible

for the enactment of all laws applicable in Western Sahara. Judicial authority would be vested in a supreme court and such other courts as might be
established by the Western Sahara Authority. Elections for the legislative
assembly and chief executive of the Authority were to be held within one
year of the effective date of the plan, and those eligible to vote would be
persons aged eighteen or over whose names appeared on the provisional
voter list (again without giving effect to any appeals or objections) or on
the UNHCR repatriation list. Eligibility would be determined by the UN,
whose decision would again be "final and without appeal."[30] Other matters
dealt with included the election and referendum campaigns, the release of
political prisoners and prisoners of war, and the reduction, confinement,
and containment of armed forces.

According to the penultimate paragraph, "The interested parties agree
that the Secretary-General shall have the authority to interpret this plan and
that in the event of any disagreement about the meaning of the plan, the
Secretary-General's interpretation shall be binding on the interested parties."[31] The final paragraph provided for the signature of the interested
parties, the neighboring countries, and the United Nations in agreement to
the terms of the plan.

Both Morocco and the Polisario provided reasoned and lengthy responses spelling out their difficulties with various provisions of the plan.
Morocco, while not rejecting the proposal, was uncomfortable with many
aspects, not least the legal system and with a referendum offering only a
choice between integration and independence instead of a negotiated compromise, "leaving, in the final analysis, a winner and a loser"; it saw the
Secretary-General's binding authority as raising "difficulties both in principle and at the technical level."[32] The Polisario was naturally concerned
about the return of refugees and their situation; after presenting critical
remarks on other details of the plan, it ended by proposing ways to revive
the settlement plan and have the outcome enforced.[33] Algeria also submitted
elaborate comments criticizing many aspects.[34] All three drew particular
attention to the crucial one-year period preceding the election of the Western
Sahara Authority. Mauritania reiterated "its full readiness to lend its backing
to any political solution that meets with the support of the parties."[35]

In his observations and recommendations the Secretary-General
addressed what he saw as Morocco's main objection: that one of only two
ballot choices should be independence. A possible amendment might be to
provide a third choice other than integration and independence offering
self-government or autonomy. He considered the Polisario's chief objection
to be that the peace plan "is not the settlement plan." The settlement plan,
being subject to the parties' "consent [not just cooperation] at every stage,"
made it difficult to envision Morocco's consenting to Polisario's suggestions
for implementing the plan; it was as difficult to imagine that the Security

Council would take action "to enforce the result of the referendum under Chapter VII." Kofi Annan was convinced that the Baker peace plan offered what could be "an optimum political solution" providing the "bona fide residents of Western Sahara . . . the opportunity to determine their own future."[36] He warned the Council against supporting a process in which objections or changes were to be negotiated with the parties, between them, or under UN auspices. The problem would not be solved "without asking that one or both of the parties do something they are not otherwise prepared to do." Short of that, the Council might "wish to consider whether it wishes to remain actively seized of this political process."[37]

As the Security Council was about to begin its deliberations, the Frente Polisario sprang a surprise. In an astute tactical move, it officially accepted the peace plan. Ahmed Bukhari, Polisario's representative at the UN, announced that "without abandoning the 1991 settlement plan, [Polisario] would be ready to contribute to the effective study of the way proposed by Mr. Baker to reach the inescapable goal of self-determination of the Sahrawi people." This was, Bukhari explained, in response to the "insistently expressed wish by many countries within and outside the Security Council such as Algeria and Spain."[38] Possibly also the United States, which wanted to back Baker. Morocco, disliking the plan and the prospect of any attempt to impose a settlement, had presumably counted on Polisario's rejection and was thoroughly bemused.

After much lobbying, the Council agreed on a resolution intended to "assist the parties to achieve a just, lasting and mutually acceptable political solution" that would provide for the self-determination of the people of Western Sahara. But the preamble went on to specify that the Council was "acting under Chapter VI of the Charter of the United Nations." In short, this remained an exercise of good offices, not binding arbitration subject to enforcement. The Council supported strongly the efforts of the Secretary-General and his personal envoy and "similarly supports their Peace plan for self-determination of the people of Western Sahara as an optimum political solution on the basis of agreement between the parties." It called on the parties to work with the UN and with each other toward acceptance and implementation of the plan.[39]

A Moroccan delegation at the ministerial level met Baker in Houston on 17 September, but Rabat refused to relinquish its "opposition to the peace plan," as the Secretary-General reported to the Council in October. In the same report, he urged Morocco to "seize the opportunity and positively engage in the process of accepting and implementing the plan," which "represents a fair and balanced approach . . . providing each side some, but perhaps not all, of what it wants."[40] Morocco reacted angrily. In a letter to the president of the Council, it accused the "Secretariat" of lacking neutrality and failing to interpret objectively the July resolution, which spoke of "agreement between the parties." There could be no question of simply signing a text without negotiation. Nor was Morocco's objection limited to one issue: it concerned the whole "architecture of the framework proposed," which derived more from the superseded settlement plan than the idea of a "third way." It appealed to the Security Council to assist the parties in reaching a "mutually acceptable solution," far from any thought of its being imposed on them. [41] The Moroccan ministry of foreign affairs and cooperation issued a communiqué reaffirming support for a "realistic political solution" that would respect the "sovereignty and territorial integrity of the Kingdom." [42]

Algeria wrote to the president of the Security Council in favor of the peace plan. It hoped that, "following the steps of the Frente Polisario, Morocco will choose to seize the opportunity . . . and . . . start to implement the plan." The July resolution was, in its view, crystal clear, and thus Algeria called on the parties "to move towards acceptance and implementation." [43]

While attending the UN General Assembly, King Mohammed VI met with President Bush and was reportedly given assurances that the United States would not impose a solution unacceptable to Morocco or have the Security Council do so. On 27 October, U.S. assistant secretary of state William Burns was received in Rabat and reaffirmed that the United States was not supportive of the imposition of a solution; he exhorted the parties to work with each other and the UN to find the means of moving forward. [44] On a state visit to Morocco, also in October, French president Jacques Chirac responded to a question concerning Western Sahara: "You know the position of France in this affair and it is our steadfast position there where the debate takes place, that is to say in the Security Council, at the UN, and it consists in supporting the position of Morocco. . . . We are of the opinion that a solution requires the agreement of the parties, more particularly the two principal parties, and that a solution cannot be imposed by the international community against the will of one of the parties." [45]

On 28 October the Security Council adopted a brief and bland resolution. Recalling previous resolutions and reaffirming "in particular, resolution 1495(2003) of 31 July 2003," it decided to extend MINURSO for three months and asked the Secretary-General to report. [46]

Notes

1. Report of the Secretary-General, S/2000/683 (12 July 2000), par. 8.
2. Ibid., par. 29.
3. Report of the Secretary-General, S/2000/1029 (25 October 2000), pars. 27, 5.
4. Ibid., par. 13.
5. Ibid., par. 30.
6. Report of the Secretary-General, S/2001/148 (20 February 2001), par. 3.
7. Ibid., par. 6.

8. Ibid., pars. 15–16.

9. Ibid., par. 22.

10. Report of the Secretary-General, S/2001/613 (20 June 2001), pars. 39, 41.

11. Ibid., par. 52.

12. Ibid., par. 55.

13. Confirmed in Report of the Secretary-General, S/2002/41 (10 January 2002), par. 3.

14. Report of the Secretary-General, S/2001/613 (20 June 2001), Annex IV.

15. Ibid., Annex II.

16. Report of the Secretary-General, S/2002/41 (10 January 2002), par. 9; Annex I, 7–8.

17. Ibid., Annex II.

18. Report of the Secretary-General, S/2002/41 (10 January 2002), par. 11.

19. Ibid., Annex III, 15–16.

20. Report of the Secretary-General, S/2002/178 (19 February 2002), pars. 40, 45.

21. Ibid., par. 44.

22. Ibid., pars. 48–51.

23. Security Council Resolution 1394 (2002), 27 February 2002.

24. Report of the Secretary-General, S/2002/467 (19 April 2002), par. 22.

25. Security Council Resolution 1429 (2002), 30 July 2002.

26. *Le Matin,* 6 November 2002.

27. Report of the Secretary-General. S/2003/565 of 23 May 2003, Annex II, 14–18.

28. Ibid., Annex III, 19–65.

29. Ibid., Annex II, par. 5.

30. Ibid., Annex II, par. 16.

31. Ibid., Annex II, par. 22.

32. Ibid., Annex III, 22, 32.

33. Ibid., 44.

34. Ibid., 45–63.

35. Ibid., Annex III, 65, par. iv.

36. Ibid., pars. 53–54, 50.

37. Ibid., pars. 56–57, 60.

38. Office of the Frente Polisario representative at the United Nations, 11 July 2003.

39. Security Council Resolution 1495(2003), 31 July 2003.

40. Report of the Secretary-General, S/2003/1016 (16 October 2003), pars. 26–27.

41. UN Document S/2003/1028, 21 October 2003.

42. Communiqué of the Ministry of Foreign Affairs and Cooperation, Rabat, 28 October 2003.

43. UN Document S/2003/1045 (28 October 2003).

44. *L'Intelligent.com,* 28 October 2003.

45. Press conference, 11 October 2003, L'Elysee website, www.elysee.fr.

46. Security Council Resolution 1513(2003), 28 October 2003.

9

Stalemate:
Who Decides the
Future of Western Sahara?

As I write, it is thirty years since the Frente Polisario came into existence, a full generation, and as long as the Cold War lasted. It is nearly thirty years since the Spanish census of 1974, with all that it was to entail. And it will soon be thirty years since the International Court of Justice gave its advisory opinion, since the Green March, since Spain's precipitous departure from the Sahara, and since the proclamation of the SADR. It is worth asking what has changed in that time and what has not.

If there is one constant, it is Morocco's claim to the territory, never mind the initial deal with Mauritania. King Hassan II asserted his right to reclaim the sometime Spanish Sahara as he did other Spanish possessions in northwest Africa. He dramatized it with the Green March. He stated it before the OAU, where his refusal to accord any recognition to the SADR led to heated confrontation within the organization and its near demise. He restated it even when conceding a referendum that would also "give justice" to "Morocco's conviction of the legitimacy of its rights." He reiterated it on numerous later occasions when referring to the "confirmatory" referendum planned under UN and OAU auspices. Equally constant were Algeria's public rejection of the Moroccan claim and its staunch support of the Polisario and the Western Saharan people's inalienable right to self-determination. However, there have been moments when it was imagined that Algeria might negotiate. Algerian domestic politics and Algeria's relations with Morocco, and the relations of both Morocco and Algeria with more powerful states, are among the key fluctuations to affect the situation.

External events intervened from the beginning when the Cold War and its alliances influenced attitudes to the confrontation in northwest Africa. Morocco was determinedly anticommunist and sympathetic to the Western-U.S. camp, while the Polisario, backed by Algeria, Libya, and Cuba, was closer to the Soviet Union. International opinion was split. On the same day in December 1975, the UN General Assembly adopted two different resolutions on Spanish Sahara. One, taking note of the Madrid tripartite agreement by which Spain ceded the territory to Morocco and Mauritania, called for the "Saharan populations originating in the Territory" to determine their future. The other studiously ignored the Madrid agreement and emphasized support for the people of Spanish Sahara's inalienable right to self-determination. As a sign of things to come, one well-intentioned, but perhaps not well-instructed, member state rationalized that the two texts were complementary and declared a vote for both resolutions.

For almost fifteen years after the Spanish withdrawal, the status of the territory was consigned to OAU in-fighting. The OAU had become overtly engaged when after only three years Mauritania was forced to relinquish its share, in effect to Morocco, but the organization was unable to muster coherent support for action. Global involvement was marginal until the Cold War ended. The fall of the Berlin Wall, U.S. president George H. W. Bush's "new world order," and the successful outcome of the campaign to expel the Iraqi invader from Kuwait generated a sense of expectation, inspiring confidence that the Maghrebian confrontation could be peacefully resolved. The UN Secretary-General presented a settlement plan for Western Sahara.

The Security Council, buoyed by the general optimism, agreed to endorse a plan about which there were serious reservations. It counted on the Secretary-General's good offices to resolve differences with the willing cooperation of the parties. Experience over the years had shown that the Secretary-General's good offices could be effective in many circumstances. Most straightforward were situations when parties to a conflict were prepared to end it but preferred to concede to a ruling of the Secretary-General. Such was the case in a border dispute between Guyana and Venezuela. In Bahrain, a potentially explosive confrontation between Iran and Arab states was defused, without loss of face, by recourse to the Secretary-General as an impartial intermediary. The Council also appreciated the Secretary-General's good offices when the great powers reached agreement on an objective but needed to act through this neutral arm. That was so in connection with the Soviet withdrawal from Afghanistan, in relation to Cambodia, in Namibia, and in Central America. In different circumstances, the Council found it convenient to entrust to the Secretary-General problems that seemed insoluble, arguably to foster the illusion of action or to shift responsibility. But common to the successful exercise of good offices was either the willingness of the parties to work toward a solution or a great power decision in the background, or both. This is not to diminish the value of the Secretary-General's role; it can be indispensable, but it is not independent of the realities of power.

If the Security Council, endorsing the Secretary-General's mission of good offices with respect to Western Sahara and "welcoming" the proposals of December 1991, accepted conflicting interpretations at the introductory stage in the expectation that these could be reconciled as implementation proceeded, it hoped in vain. The positions of the parties were as rigid as they were incompatible. Division in the General Assembly was enough to enable Morocco to maintain that its presence in Western Sahara, following the Madrid Accords, had been tacitly accepted and that any referendum could only be decided by all the "Saharan populations originating in the Territory." The Polisario, supported by Algeria, was equally able to argue that the General Assembly had called for an unequivocal act of self-determination by the "people of Spanish Sahara."

Perez de Cuellar's memoirs show that he had doubts about aspects of the settlement plan, and Boutros-Ghali repeatedly hinted to the Security Council that it might consider an alternative way forward. They recognized what both Morocco and the Polisario knew: that the plan's core was the electoral roll of who was to vote for or against integration with Morocco or independence. It was formulated as an either-or choice, and the composition of the roll would be decisive. From the outset, Polisario insisted on a restrictive interpretation tied to the 1974 census, which it calculated to serve its cause. Morocco was equally adamant that only a much more comprehensive view of who should vote would be true to historical and social reality and, of course, ensure a confirmatory referendum. Neither wavered. Polisario had the advantage of a census listing and documents; Morocco relied on oral testimony and the shaikhs. The identification of tens of thousands of applicants from the contested groupings was doomed to failure. Polisario rejected these as fully Western Saharan tribes; it did not have the relevant shaikhs to present nor the necessary tribal knowledge, and even in cases where there existed acceptable alternates, it was sure to reject such applicants. Morocco could hardly allow all those applications to lapse, nor could it alter the verdict. When the contested groups were rejected in the thousands, almost in their entirety, Morocco denounced the process. MINURSO was made responsible for the failure of identification to deliver what Morocco needed. As identification eventually ended, the Polisario had what it had always sought and saw every reason to push ahead with the referendum. Morocco was not about to let that happen.

There never was a moment when the process could deliver a result that was politically acceptable to both sides and that both would willingly implement. Yet the Security Council countenanced ambiguity and called on the parties to cooperate voluntarily. From the beginning there was no strong mandate, no demand that the parties comply with a decisive plan of action. Hassan II ignored the appeal to desist from marching into Spanish Sahara at the time of the Green March. Once entrenched in a region he staunchly characterized as historically Moroccan, he was not about to withdraw of his own free will. Nor was his son and heir. As time passed, in the Security

Council's many subsequent resolutions it never mentioned sanctions, intimated coercion, nor as much as hinted at the use of force to compel compliance. Even when James Baker, with U.S. backing, urged the Council to select one option and impose it, the Council demurred. When the Baker peace plan sought to eliminate the prospect of endless negotiation, the divided Council reiterated its commitment to an exercise of good offices under Chapter VI of the UN Charter.

That identification proceeded to the bitter end proved a mixed blessing. The polarized conclusion did little to encourage negotiation. In 1996, there had been sufficient pointers to the likely outcome but sufficient uncertainty to stimulate some willingness to compromise, in keeping with the Baker prescription that would provide each side with some, but perhaps not all, of what it wanted. An opportunity was lost for reasons unrelated to Western Sahara. Instead, the settlement plan staggered on only to be superseded after twelve long years—even though the Polisario declared itself willing to consider the Baker peace plan always "without abandoning the 1991 settlement plan."

The plan as originally endorsed by the Security Council failed in many respects, but in some it succeeded. Apart from identification, which (over)achieved its stated purpose, there has been peaceable interaction between the two sides, and most important, the cease-fire has held. That is a great accomplishment, though not without unintended consequences. It has saved lives, which is much to its credit. On the other hand, by halting hostilities, it let Western Sahara slip beneath the horizon of international awareness and made a solution seem less imperative. It removed the incentive to compromise that arises when fighting leads to exhaustion and grows too costly, so that an alternative becomes appealing. Continuing confrontation without military engagement may have suited Algeria as an expensive irritant to Morocco, though Morocco enjoyed having a large army, deployed away from the capital, and benefited as the controlling power in the territory and from the passage of time. The Polisario, waiting in refugee camps and largely dependent on relief supplies, had been counting on disruption to follow the death of King Hassan II, only to be faced with a stable transfer of power to Mohammed VI and the orderly replacement of the powerful Driss Basri, former minister of interior.

Relative calm enabled the media and international opinion to ignore the conflict. The major powers were under little or no pressure to act. Although historically and emotionally Spain is more closely involved, only two states have important interests in northwest Africa and the real potential to affect events. France, with investments, markets, and traditional ties, is profoundly concerned about the impact of any disruptive change on the population of the region and its countrymen abroad, largely in France. The United States has strategic, economic, and other interests, not least in the war on terrorism, which would be threatened by instability; Morocco has already proved itself a reliable ally in combating terrorists. The United States and France are, of course, two out of five permanent members of the Security Council. Neither has shown any disposition to bring serious pressure to bear on Morocco, obliging it to implement an act of self-determination on terms that Morocco deems dangerous to its stability and integrity, much less countenanced expelling Morocco by force from Western Sahara.

It is difficult to see the Baker peace plan being forced on Morocco and as difficult to imagine that Morocco would accept it without pressure. (Richard Holbrooke, a propos of Bosnia, reportedly said that negotiation without the credible threat of force is useless.) As it stands, the proposal is astutely structured to accommodate, in the first stage, the electoral roll emerging from identification and welcomed by Polisario and, at the second stage, the expanded and larger population presumed favorable to Morocco. It does not clearly address what would happen during the first year—a point of concern to Polisario, Algeria, and Morocco—but that is less fraught than the prospect of four years of cohabitation under what could well be Polisario-dominated leadership of refugees who have returned from Tindouf and the more numerous, predominantly ex-Morocco, population already established in the territory, who will have Morocco ready to help them defend their interests. The Polisario leaders, before I left in 1998, spoke of the "Sahrawis" as "a minority in their own country." The tension, after years—in the case of the younger generation a lifetime—of prolonged deprivation and profound mistrust, could all too easily erupt into civil conflict, defying control in a vast desert area replete with arms and military experience and drawing in foreign sympathizers.

The World Court opinion, while recognizing historical ties of allegiance between some tribal leaders in Western Sahara and the Moroccan sovereign, upheld the people's right to the free and genuine expression of their will. Self-determination is an almost sacrosanct principle with the UN General Assembly and at the OAU/AU (which is also officially committed to colonial frontiers, however arbitrary). It has motivated international involvement for all these years. However, self-determination, as James Baker pointed out and the Secretary-General reported to the Security Council, can take various forms. It can be achieved by war or revolution, through elections—which require goodwill—or agreement. The path as mapped in the settlement plan was not the only option. The latest "peace plan" is another. Even if there are serious doubts about the draft as presented, it provides a basis, or at least an impetus, for negotiation. Negotiation is inevitable if the Council refuses to impose a solution, though without the credible threat of force, it could be painfully long. On the other hand, a return to hostilities cannot be the way to solve the problem. War would generate more suffering and more refugees, would disrupt the region and probably enlarge the conflict.

The more time passes, the more questions arise about the electoral roll. It is pointless to speculate about the outcome had there been an act of self-determination as originally envisaged by Spain or immediately following the advisory opinion and as called for by the General Assembly. By the time the Security Council took action, the situation on the ground had already changed. It has continued to change ever since. The population of Western Sahara is not the same as under Spanish colonial rule, and it is many times larger. The longer it takes to reach a negotiated solution, the more significant the demographic shift will be. That cannot but make the 1974 census increasingly less relevant as a principal reference. The decade since 1993 already calls for further revision of the revised list as people die, and the 31 December deadline of that year by which applicants had to be eighteen years of age cannot be valid forever. Although one of the Secretary-General's December 1991 criteria, which infuriated Polisario at the time, specified six years' residence "prior to 1975" as a qualification (in addition to Saharan tribal membership), the day approaches when others with six or more years' residence will demand their say, not only as in Baker's second round.

In June 2004, James Baker informed the Secretary-General that he believed he had done all he could on the issue and offered his resignation as personal envoy. Kofi Annan accepted the resignation with deep regret and advised the Security Council accordingly.

*   *   *

Morocco needs legitimacy; it would welcome international recognition of its place in the former Spanish Sahara. What it is willing to concede to that end is another matter. Even a Saharan vote favoring regional autonomy could make Rabat nervous about the potential implications for certain regions of the kingdom. Other Saharan concerns have a domestic Moroccan dimension. While the passage of time may seem politically advantageous, 140,000 men under (expensive) arms take a heavy toll on the budget, only partially offset by the challenge to a society lacking full employment opportunities if obliged to absorb demobilized youngish men in their tens of thousands. The privileges accorded settlers in Western Sahara and the benefits that the territory enjoys come at the expense of needs elsewhere for investment in infrastructure, education, and social services. Discovery of oil for extraction in commercially viable quantities by the companies currently active off shore would promise revenue, but it might complicate any solution by raising the stakes.

Of comparable significance to Moroccan domestic politics are Algerian policies. Algeria will have a codetermining role in any settlement. It seems iniquitous that in this equation the Frente Polisario is reduced in status. Its people have fought for their cause with courage, dignity, and determination but have always been dependent on forces greater than themselves. Their resilience and discipline are impressive, and even if some refugee families are tempted to join fellow Sahrawis in Mauritania or relatives in Western Sahara, the leaders may want to soldier on. But they cannot defeat Morocco militarily, and in the current climate, armed incursions threatening regional stability will make them few friends. The United States seeks stability in northwest Africa. A U.S. presidency waging a global war on terrorism is disposed to sympathize with a moderately conservative Arab-Muslim country that discourages fundamentalism and cooperates in combating terrorists.

Fifteen years since the Cold War ended, another global confrontation casts its shadow over Western Sahara. The prospect of a peaceful resolution of the conflict remains elusive, prolonging the pain of those who survive in refugee camps with ever-diminishing hope. The core question is still: Who will decide the future of Western Sahara?

Appendix 1

The Situation Concerning Western Sahara: Report of the Secretary-General S/21360 of 18 June 1990

General Introduction

1. On 11 August 1988, the Secretary-General of the United Nations and the Special Envoy of the then Chairman of the Assembly of Heads of State and Government of the Organization of African Unity (OAU) presented, in separate meetings, to the parties to the conflict in Western Sahara, namely Morocco and the Frente Popular para la Liberación de Saguia el-Hamra y de Río de Oro (Frente POLISARIO), a document ("the settlement proposals") containing proposals for a just and definitive solution of the question of Western Sahara in conformity with General Assembly resolution 1514 (XV) by means of a cease-fire and the holding of a referendum without military or administrative constraints to enable the people of Western Sahara, in the exercise of their right to self-determination, to choose between independence and integration with Morocco.

2. On 30 August 1988, in separate meetings, the representatives of each of the two parties, while making comments and observations, informed the Secretary-General of their agreement in principle to the settlement proposals. On 20 September 1988 the Security Council was informed of this fact by the Secretary-General who provided the Council with an outline of the settlement proposals. The Council thereupon adopted resolution 621 (1988) of 20 September 1988, authorizing the Secretary-General to appoint a special representative for Western Sahara and requesting him to transmit to it as soon as possible a report on the holding of a referendum for self-determination of the people of Western Sahara and on ways and means to ensure the organization and supervision of such a referendum by the United Nations in co-operation with OAU.

3. The present report is divided into two parts:

> (a) Part I contains the full text of the settlement proposals as accepted in principle by the parties on 30 August 1988. The Secretary-General

believes that it would be useful for the Council to have the full text available to it at this stage, thus supplementing the outline he had provided to the Council in 1988;

(b) Part II contains a report on developments since September 1988 and it contains the Secretary-General's implementation plan for giving effect to the settlement proposals, taking account of developments since their acceptance in principle by the parties. The implementation plan is submitted to the Council pursuant to its request contained in resolution 621 (1988).

Part I: Proposals by the Secretary-General of the United Nations and the Current Chairman of the Assembly of Heads of State and Government of the Organization of African Unity Aimed at a Settlement of the Question of Western Sahara Accepted in Principle by the Parties on 30 August 1988

I. Introduction

4. The essential aim of the proposals by the Secretary-General of the United Nations and the current Chairman of OAU is to enable the people of the Territory of Western Sahara to exercise their right to self-determination and independence, in accordance with United Nations General Assembly resolutions 1514 (XV) of 14 December 1960 and 40/50 of 2 December 1985 and resolution AHG/Res. 104 (XIX) adopted by the Assembly of Heads of State and Government of OAU at its nineteenth ordinary session held at Addis Ababa from 6 to 12 June 1983. To this end, the Secretary-General of the United Nations and the current Chairman of the OAU have held consultations with the two parties to the conflict in Western Sahara, Morocco and the Frente Popular para la Liberación de Saquía el-Hamra y de Río de Oro (Frente POLISARIO), aimed at promoting the conclusion of an agreement on the organization of a fair and impartial referendum, without military or administrative constraints.

5. The Secretary-General of the United Nations and the current Chairman of OAU believe that the following proposals represent a compromise and a practical and reasonable basis for implementing OAU resolution AHG/Res. 104 (XIX) and General Assembly resolution 40/50, while taking the two parties' interests into account.

6. To this end, they have drawn up proposals for settling the question of Western Sahara that would enable the people of the Territory to exercise their inalienable right to self-determination and independence under conditions acceptable to them and, hence, to the international community.

II. Role of the Security Council

7. The Security Council will be called on to adopt a resolution requesting the Secretary-General to appoint a special representative. The Secretary-General will make this appointment in consultation with the current Chairman of OAU and with the consent of the parties to the conflict. The Security Council will make the necessary arrangements for the deployment of the Observer Group mentioned in paragraphs 12, 16, 17, 18 (d) and 20 below.

III. Mandate and Functions of the Special Representative of the Secretary-General

8. During the transitional period lasting from the entry into force of the cease-fire to the announcement of the results of the referendum, the Special Representative will have sole and exclusive authority over all matters relating to the referendum, its organization and conduct.

9. The Special Representative will be assisted by a Support Group made available to him by the Secretary-General of the United Nations and large enough to enable him to perform his organizational and supervisory functions. This Group will include a civilian unit, a military unit and a security unit. The Special Representative and the Support Group will make up the United Nations provisional administration during the transitional period.

10. In order to carry out fully and effectively the mandate and functions entrusted to him, the Special Representative will have the power to take any action he deems necessary to guarantee the freedom of movement and the security of the population, as well as the impartiality of the referendum. To this end, he will have the authority to take, on the spot, any administrative, technical or security measures which he deems it appropriate to apply in the Territory during the transitional period. Such measures will concern matters relating to the conduct of the referendum campaign, such as political meetings and publicity. The Special Representative of the Secretary-General will also be able to request the suspension of any law or measure which, in his view, might hinder the smooth conduct of a free and equitable referendum. Any dispute arising between the parties to the conflict and the Special Representative will have to be submitted to the Secretary-General of the United Nations for a decision.

IV. Cease-Fire

A. Cease-fire declaration

11. In conformity with the relevant provisions of General Assembly resolutions 1514 (XV) and 40/50 and OAU resolution AHG/Res. 104 (XIX),

the parties to the conflict in Western Sahara, Morocco and the Frente POLISARIO, undertake to end all acts of hostility and to abide scrupulously by the cease-fire to be declared by the Secretary-General of the United Nations, in consultation with the current Chairman of OAU, at a date and in accordance with the procedures set forth below.

B. Date and procedures for the cease-fire

12. As soon as he receives notification from the two parties that they agree to the present proposals, the Secretary-General of the United Nations will send identical letters to Morocco and the Frente POLISARIO proposing a date and a time for the entry into force of the cease-fire. In the letter, which will form an integral part of the present proposals, the Secretary-General of the United Nations will ask the two parties to notify him in writing of their readiness to abide by the terms of the cease-fire. He will also ask the two parties to notify him of their agreement to the proposed date, four weeks prior to the entry into force of the cease-fire. This period is necessary to give the two parties time to inform their troops of the date and exact time at which the cease-fire will take effect and to permit the deployment of the United Nations Observer Group mentioned in paragraphs 16, 17, 18 (d) and 20 below. The Secretary-General of the United Nations will keep the current Chairman of OAU informed of developments in the situation and will inform him as soon as he receives notification from the two parties that they agree to the terms of the cease-fire.

13. The parties to the conflict undertake to refrain from any act which might lead to hostilities during the period between the date when the Secretary-General of the United Nations receives their reply and the date when the cease-fire takes effect.

14. Immediately after the cease-fire has been declared, the parties to the conflict will halt all their military operations, including troop movements and reinforcements, and acts of violence or intimidation.

15. One week before the entry into force of the cease-fire, the parties to the conflict will notify the Special Representative of the Secretary-General of the United Nations of the size of their forces deployed.

16. So that a referendum may be organized without military constraints, Morocco undertakes to effect an appropriate, substantial and phased reduction of its troops in Western Sahara. The Moroccan troop reduction will be followed immediately by the deployment of the United Nations Observer Group in the Territory. The remaining troops, whose numbers must not exceed . . . men, will be confined to locations designated by the Special Representative of the Secretary-General of the United Nations, and will be placed under the supervision of the United Nations Observer Group.

17. The Frente POLISARIO likewise undertakes to have all its troops confined, under the supervision of the United Nations Observer Group, to

locations indicated to it by the Special Representative of the Secretary-General of the United Nations. The Moroccan troops and the Frente POLISARIO troops will be confined simultaneously. The confinement of the troops, together with their weapons and equipment, will be completed . . . days after the date of entry into force of the cease-fire.

18. The parties to the conflict undertake scrupulously to observe a complete cessation of all acts of hostility so that the referendum process will be free of any interference or intimidation. The Special Representative will take measures concerning: (a) observance of the cessation of all acts of hostility; (b) military arrangements for the Support Group; and (c) military arrangements for the troops of the parties. Such measures include:

(a) The cessation of all hostilities by the two parties, and the confinement of the armed forces of Morocco and the Frente POLISARIO, as called for in paragraphs 16 and 17 above;

(b) The phased reduction of Moroccan troops in Western Sahara, with the exception of (number to be specified) of them, within a period of 12 weeks and before the official opening of the referendum campaign. The freedom of movement of the Moroccan forces remaining in the Territory will be restricted to the locations referred to in paragraph 16, and these forces will be withdrawn from the Territory 24 hours after the results of the voting are confirmed, if the outcome of the referendum so requires;

(c) The freedom of movement of the Frente POLISARIO forces will be restricted to the locations referred to in paragraph 17, and these forces will be disbanded 24 hours after the results of the voting are confirmed, if the outcome of the referendum so requires;

(d) The neutralization of Morocco's paramilitary forces by the United Nations Observer Group;

(e) Arrangements enabling members of the Frente POLISARIO who are outside the Territory to return to Western Sahara without hindrance, peacefully and unarmed, via entry points designated by the Special Representative, in order to participate freely in the referendum;

(f) The stipulation that the military unit of the Support Group will ensure that the parties comply with any provisions deriving from the outcome of the referendum.

19. The Special Representative will ensure that all the above measures are properly implemented.

20. The Secretary-General of the United Nations, after consulting the Security Council, will appoint a United Nations observer group to be stationed in Western Sahara. The Observer Group will be established and will

function in accordance with the general principles applicable to United Nations peace-keeping operations. The Group will be large enough and its composition sufficiently broad for it to be able to perform the functions envisaged in the present proposals. The Group will be responsible for supervising the cessation of hostilities, the application of the cease-fire, the provision of supplies to the troops of the parties to the conflict and the exchange of prisoners. The Observer Group will also be responsible for ascertaining the respective positions of the forces of the two parties at the moment when the cease-fire takes effect. The exchange of prisoners will take place under the supervision of the Observer Group no later than . . . days after the cease-fire begins.

21. Morocco and the Frente POLISARIO undertake to co-operate fully with the Observer Group and to abide by and observe scrupulously the above cease-fire provisions.

22. Algeria and Mauritania also undertake to co-operate fully with the Observer Group and to abide by and observe scrupulously the above cease-fire provisions.

V. Referendum

23. In conformity with OAU resolution AHG/Res. 104 (XIX) and General Assembly resolutions 1514 (XV) and 40/50, a referendum will be organized in Western Sahara to enable the people of the Territory to decide their own future freely and democratically. The referendum will be organized and conducted by the United Nations, in co-operation with OAU, during a transitional period.

A. Census of the Saharan population

24. All Saharans counted in the 1974 census taken by the Spanish authorities and aged 18 years or over will have the right to vote in the referendum. With the assistance of the United Nations High Commissioner for Refugees (UNHCR), a census of Saharan refugees living outside the Territory will be taken in places designated by the Special Representative.

25. To facilitate the task of taking a census of the Saharan populations the Secretary-General will set up, in consultation with the current Chairman of OAU, an identification commission responsible for carefully and scrupulously reviewing the 1974 census and updating it. Under the authority of the Special Representative of the Secretary-General, the Commission will perform its task during the transitional period. In any case, it must have completed its work before the referendum campaign begins.

26. The Identification Commission will consist of a population expert familiar with the problems and features of Saharan society, assisted by

three to five specialists in the demographics of countries whose population is predominantly nomadic. The Commission will form an integral part of the Support Group of the Special Representative of the Secretary-General.

27. The role of the Saharan Identification Commission will be:

(a) To review carefully the census taken in the Territory in 1974 by the Spanish authorities and update it;

(b) Calculate the real growth of the Saharan population in the period between the date of the above census and the date of organization of the referendum, taking into account the following elements:

(i) Births and deaths;

(ii) Movements of the Saharan population.

28. On the basis of the information mentioned above, the Identification Commission will establish as precisely as possible the number of Saharans living in the Territory of Western Sahara and the number of Saharan refugees and non-residents qualified to participate in the referendum.

29. The Saharan Identification Commission will function as follows:

(a) In the first stage, the Identification Commission will conduct its research under the guidance of the population expert, who will submit reports to the Special Representative on the progress of the Commission's work;

(b) In the second stage, once its preliminary research is complete, the Identification Commission will meet in the presence of the tribal chiefs of Western Sahara. The chiefs will be asked to comment on and contribute to the work of the Identification Commission;

(c) The representatives of the two parties and of OAU mentioned in paragraph 37 of the present document will also be invited to attend, as observers, meetings of the Identification Commission held with the Saharan tribal chiefs.

30. The Saharan Identification Commission will transmit the results and conclusions of its work to the Special Representative, who will submit them to the Secretary-General for consideration in consultation with the current Chairman of OAU.

B. Procedures for the referendum

31. The people of Western Sahara will choose, freely and democratically, between independence and integration with Morocco.

32. Voting will be by secret ballot. Arrangements will be made for people who cannot read or write.

33. The following conditions will have to be met to the satisfaction of the Special Representative of the Secretary-General, in order to guarantee the organization of a free and equitable referendum:

   (a) Before the referendum campaign begins, the Special Representative of the Secretary-General may, if he considers it necessary and in the manner envisaged in paragraph 10 above, cause the suspension of any law or measure which, in his view, might limit or prevent the achievement of this objective;

   (b) The Special Representative, in co-operation with the parties to the conflict, will take steps to ensure that all Saharan political prisoners and detainees are released before the beginning of the referendum campaign, so that they can participate freely and without restriction in the referendum. Any dispute concerning the release of political prisoners and detainees must be settled to the satisfaction of the Special Representative, who will be assisted in this task by an independent legal expert appointed by the Secretary-General of the United Nations;

   (c) All Saharan refugees counted in the census taken pursuant to paragraph 24 above will be able to return freely to the Territory and participate without restriction in the referendum, without running the risk of arrest, detention, intimidation or imprisonment. Various entry points will be designated for this purpose by the Special Representative;

   (d) With the assistance of the United Nations High Commissioner for Refugees, the Special Representative will make sure that Saharans residing outside the Territory are able to choose freely and voluntarily whether or not to return to the Territory;

   (e) The referendum campaign will begin only when the Special Representative is satisfied that the procedure governing the referendum is equitable and can be applied.

34. The Special Representative will rule quickly on the starting date of the referendum campaign, the preparation of the registers of voters and any other procedural matter, in order to give all Saharans, without restriction and in complete equity, the opportunity to participate in the campaign. Complete freedom of speech, assembly, movement and the press will be guaranteed.

35. The Special Representative of the Secretary-General will be responsible for maintaining law and order in Western Sahara during the transitional period. The Special Representative will also ensure that no one can resort to intimidation or interfere in the referendum process.

36. At each stage of the referendum, the Special Representative will make sure that all the provisions and guarantees of the present document are being respected.

37. The Special Representative of the Secretary-General will invite the representatives of the two parties to the conflict in Western Sahara to observe the organization and conduct of the referendum, without prejudice to his exclusive authority as provided for in the present document. Should these observers have any complaints, they will submit them directly to the Special Representative, whose decision thereon will be final.

38. The two parties to the conflict undertake to co-operate fully with the Special Representative of the Secretary-General in the performance of his functions.

39. The Special Representative will also invite the representatives of OAU to observe the organization and conduct of the referendum, without prejudice to his authority as provided for in the present document. They may submit any observations they might have directly to the Special Representative, who will take whatever action he deems appropriate.

40. Morocco and the Frente POLISARIO undertake to accept and abide by the results of the referendum.

41. As soon as the results of the referendum have been certified by the Special Representative, the Secretary-General will notify the current Chairman of OAU and the United Nations Security Council and will take the necessary steps to give effect to the decision of the Saharan people as expressed in the referendum.

42. The neighbouring countries, Algeria and Mauritania, will do their utmost to ensure that the transitional arrangements and the results of the referendum are respected. They will make available to the Special Representative and the Support Group all the material resources they need in order to be able to perform their task and to facilitate the adoption of measures relating to security and order in the border regions.

Part II: Implementation Plan Proposed by the Secretary-General Pursuant to Security Council Resolution 621 (1988) of 20 September 1988

I. Introduction

43. In its resolution 621 (1988) concerning the situation in Western Sahara the Security Council authorized the Secretary-General to appoint a special representative for Western Sahara. The Secretary-General accordingly appointed Mr. Hector Gros Espiell as his Special Representative with effect from 19 October 1988. Upon his resignation, Mr. Gros Espiell was succeeded by Mr. Johannes Manz with effect from 19 January 1990.

44. The Secretary-General also undertook preparation of the report called for in Security Council resolution 621 (1988). Having taken note of

the comments and observations made by the two parties in their acceptance of the settlement proposals and after further consultations with them and with the current Chairman of OAU, the Secretary-General, on 30 June 1989, established a technical commission at United Nations Headquarters, under his chairmanship, to study ways and means of implementing the settlement proposals. On 12 July 1989, the Special Representative handed to representatives of the two parties a draft timetable for the implementation of the settlement proposals, which had been prepared by the Technical Commission. Morocco's response to the draft timetable was received on 6 October 1989 and that of Frente POLISARIO a week later.

45. The Secretary-General has carefully studied the responses of the parties, as well as the recommendations of the Technical Commission. On the basis of this information, the Secretary-General, after consultations with the current Chairman of OAU, has come to the conclusion that the settlement proposals for Western Sahara should be implemented by means of the implementation plan contained in the present report.

46. The plan is to be carried out by the United Nations in co-operation with OAU, the representatives of which will be associated with the process throughout as official observers who may submit their observations at any stage to the Special Representative of the Secretary-General for his consideration and such action as he deems appropriate. The plan is based essentially on the provisions of the settlement proposals and attempts to meet, to the greatest extent possible, the major concerns of the parties as expressed to the Secretary-General and to the Chairman of OAU during the course of consultations over the past five years. Since presenting the settlement proposals to the parties, the Secretary-General has had further meetings with them and has provided them with additional clarification on points of particular concern to them.

II. Main Elements of the Implementation Plan

47. The implementation plan contained in the present report provides for a transitional period during which:

(a) The Special Representative of the Secretary-General, acting under the authority of the Secretary-General and, as necessary, on instructions from and in consultation with him, will have sole and exclusive responsibility over all matters relating to the referendum, including its organization and conduct;

(b) The Special Representative will be assisted by a United Nations support group, including civilian, military and security (civil police) units, made available by the Secretary-General and large enough to enable the Special Representative to perform his organizational and supervisory functions;

(c) There will be a cease-fire monitored by United Nations military personnel, followed by an exchange of prisoners of war under the auspices of the International Committee of the Red Cross (ICRC);

(d) Morocco will undertake an appropriate, substantial and phased reduction of its troops in the Territory;

(e) The combatants on each side will be confined to certain locations specified by the Special Representative where they will be monitored by United Nations military personnel;

(f) The United Nations will organize and conduct a referendum, and issue the necessary regulations, rules and instructions for this purpose, in which the people of Western Sahara will choose between independence or integration with Morocco;

(g) The United Nations will monitor other aspects of the administration of the Territory, especially the maintenance of law and order, to ensure that the necessary conditions exist for the holding of a free and fair referendum;

(h) Following on the proclamation of an amnesty, political prisoners will be released and all laws or regulations which, in the view of the Special Representative, could impede the holding of a free and fair referendum will be suspended to the extent the Special Representative deems this to be necessary;

(i) All refugees and other Western Saharans resident outside the Territory and wishing to return will be enabled to do so by the United Nations, after the latter has established their right to vote;

(j) The referendum should be held 24 weeks after the cease-fire comes into effect and its results should be proclaimed within 72 hours. The Special Representative will have the authority to determine whether circumstances require any alteration in these deadlines;

(k) Algeria and Mauritania will, as they have already indicated to the Secretary-General, co-operate with the Special Representative in ensuring that the transitional arrangements and the results of the referendum are respected.

The detailed modalities for carrying out the above elements in the implementation plan are described in the following paragraphs.

III. The Special Representative and the United Nations Mission for the Referendum in Western Sahara

48. The Special Representative, appointed by the Secretary-General pursuant to Security Council resolution 621 (1988), will be his representative in

Western Sahara for the implementation of the mandate to be conferred on the Secretary-General by the Security Council. The Special Representative, acting under the authority of the Secretary-General as described in paragraph 47 (a) above, will carry out the tasks provided for him in the settlement proposals and the present implementation plan. The Special Representative will ensure that all elements of the proposals and plan are complied with and he will, at all times, act in accordance with the terms of the proposals and the plan.

49. The Special Representative will be assisted in his tasks by a deputy special representative and by an integrated group of United Nations civilian, military and civil police personnel which he will head and direct. This group will be known as the United Nations Mission for the Referendum in Western Sahara (MINURSO). Arrangements concerning the status of MINURSO and its personnel will be made with the parties and with neighbouring States involved in the implementation of the settlement proposals. Further information on the proposed composition and tasks of the units comprising MINURSO is to be found in paragraphs 77 to 82 below.

IV. Transitional Period

50. The transitional period will begin with the coming into effect of the cease-fire and end with the proclamation of the results of the referendum. However, the United Nations would continue to have responsibilities for monitoring either the withdrawal of Moroccan troops or the demobilization of Frente POLISARIO troops, depending on the outcome of the referendum. The discharge of these responsibilities could take from four to six weeks (see para. 75 below). Thereafter, the United Nations will require a further period of four weeks to effect the withdrawal of its personnel and equipment from the Territory. MINURSO's presence in the Territory is thus expected to last for up to 35 weeks from the coming into effect of the cease-fire, subject to the authority given to the Special Representative to determine whether circumstances require any alteration in the timing of the referendum (see para. 47 (j) above).

V. Cease-Fire

51. When the Security Council has authorized the establishment of MINURSO, the Secretary-General will address identical letters to Morocco and Frente POLISARIO proposing a date and time ("D-Day") for the entry into force of the cease-fire. On D-Day the parties will cease all military operations, including troop movements (except as required or permitted under paras. 54 to 57 below) and any strengthening of positions. The date proposed for D-Day will be approximately 14 weeks after the date of the

dispatch of the Secretary-General's letters. This timing is dictated by the need to ensure that the Military Unit of MINURSO which will monitor the parties' compliance with the cease-fire will be effectively deployed throughout its area of operations by the time the cease-fire comes into effect.

52. In his letters, therefore, the Secretary-General will ask the parties to confirm in writing by a specified date that they accept both the terms of the cease-fire and the date and time proposed. The parties will also be asked to undertake to refrain from any act which could lead to hostilities during the period between their acceptance of the cease-fire and its coming into effect.

53. After the cease-fire has come into effect, the Military Unit of MINURSO will report any violation thereof immediately to the Special Representative. The Special Representative will take the matter up with the party or parties concerned and, as necessary, report to the Secretary-General, who may bring the violation to the attention of the Security Council for such action as the Council may think fit.

VI. Moroccan Military Presence

54. To permit the holding of a referendum without military constraints, Morocco has agreed to make an appropriate, substantial and phased reduction of its troops in the Territory during the transitional period, to a level acceptable to the Secretary-General. This reduction will be effected within a period of 12 weeks beginning on D-Day. At the end of the 12-week period the Military Unit of MINURSO will verify that the Moroccan troop strength in the Territory does not exceed the accepted level.

VII. Confinement of Each Party's Combatants to Agreed Locations

55. One week before D-Day each party will inform the Secretary-General of the strength and location of its military forces. With effect from D-Day the troops of each party, together with their arms and military equipment, will be confined to the locations described in paragraphs 56 and 57 below, plus any additional locations which may be determined by the Special Representative after consulting the parties. The troops' confinement to these locations will be monitored by the Military Unit of MINURSO. No movement outside the agreed locations will be permitted except for the purpose specified in paragraph 54 above or for routine logistic purposes or rotation, for which the authority of the Military Unit of MINURSO will be required in each case. The Special Representative will deal with any violation of the agreed arrangements in the manner described in paragraph 53 above.

56. The Moroccan troops remaining in the Territory will, with the exceptions mentioned in this paragraph, consist only of troops deployed in static or defensive positions along the sand wall constructed by Morocco close to the eastern and southern frontiers of the Territory. All intervention forces and artillery units will have been withdrawn, as will all Moroccan air force units previously used for interdiction and offensive operations. The only exceptions to these arrangements will be:

(a) Certain logistic and support units required to support the Moroccan troops deployed along the sand wall, and not exceeding a level acceptable to the Secretary-General, will remain deployed at their present locations at Laayoune, Dakhla and Smara; they will not, however, carry weapons in the towns or circulate there in uniform, whether on or off duty;

(b) The Moroccan air force will continue to provide meteorological services, air traffic control and radio communications within the Territory but will retain only those aircraft that are essential for the logistic support of the Moroccan troops remaining in the Territory;

(c) The Moroccan navy will continue to perform such tasks as coastal patrolling.

All the above activities will be closely monitored by the Military Unit of MINURSO.

57. Frente POLISARIO troops will be confined to locations to be designated before D-Day by the Special Representative and their activities will be closely monitored by the Military Unit of MINURSO. In this regard, the Governments of Algeria and Mauritania have indicated their readiness to co-operate with the Special Representative.

VIII. Organization and Conduct of the Referendum

58. In the settlement proposals the parties recognize that sole and exclusive responsibility for the organization and conduct of the referendum is vested in the United Nations. They have thus accepted the authority of the Organization to take the legislative and administrative steps necessary to accomplish this purpose. The Secretary-General will issue regulations to be given effect in the Territory by all concerned which essentially embody the relevant provisions of the settlement proposals agreed to by the parties. Additionally, these regulations will authorize the Special Representative, and relevant components of MINURSO acting with his consent, to issue rules and instructions, consistent with the regulations, which give detailed effect to the regulations. The regulations, rules and instructions will provide the fundamental basis for the organization and conduct of the referendum

and will thus, to the extent of any incompatibility, prevail over existing laws or measures in force in the Territory.

59. The responsibility of the United Nations in respect of the referendum can be divided into three main areas:

(a) The identification and registration of those eligible to vote;
(b) The establishment of the conditions and modalities for a referendum campaign in which freedom of speech, assembly, movement and the press are guaranteed;
(c) The conduct of the voting in a manner permitting participation by all eligible voters, without interference or intimidation, and ensuring the secrecy of the ballot.

A. Identification commission

60. To assist the Special Representative in fulfilling his responsibilities with regard to the identification and registration of those eligible to vote, the Secretary-General will appoint and issue terms of reference for an identification commission, including demographic experts, in whose work the parties and the representatives of OAU will, as appropriate, participate as official observers. The tribal chiefs of Western Sahara will also meet with the Identification Commission to contribute to its work.

B. Identification and registration of voters

61. Under the terms of the settlement proposals the Identification Commission will implement the agreed position of the parties that all Western Saharans counted in the 1974 census undertaken by the Spanish authorities and aged 18 years or over will have the right to vote, whether currently present in the Territory or outside as refugees or for other reasons. The Identification Commission, which may set up Sub-Commissions to discharge its functions in the various registration districts into which the Territory and the refugee camps will be divided, is required to update the census to provide a current basis for issuing lists of qualified voters.

62. At various stages of its work the lists prepared by the Commission will be published in the Territory and outside in areas where refugees and other Western Saharans are gathered and arrangements made for challenges to the inclusion or exclusion of any names. Any person identified as qualified to vote will at the same time be issued with a voter registration card. When the Commission has completed its compilation of the lists of those eligible to vote they will be submitted to the Secretary-General, through the Special Representative, for consideration in consultation with the current Chairman of OAU. Final lists will be issued when these are authorized by the Secretary-General. It is envisaged that the Identification Commission

will complete its work before the beginning of the referendum campaign, that is by D-Day plus 18 weeks.

C. Referendum commission

63. To assist the Special Representative in all other aspects of the organization and conduct of the referendum, the Secretary-General will appoint and issue terms of reference for a referendum commission. The Commission may establish Sub-Commissions to undertake particular responsibilities, and may co-opt as members experts in the particular subjects assigned to the Sub-Commission concerned. As in the case of the Identification Commission, representatives of the parties and of OAU will be associated with the work of the Commission and its Sub-Commissions in the capacity of official observers. In view of its responsibilities to advise on the day-to-day planning of the referendum, the Referendum Commission should commence its work as soon as possible after the Security Council has authorized the establishment of MINURSO.

D. Referendum campaign

64. As far as the establishment of the conditions and modalities for the conduct of the referendum campaign are concerned, the Referendum Commission will advise the Special Representative on the measures necessary to ensure a referendum that is free and fair, without military or administrative constraints. Such measures would include those necessary to:

(a) Guarantee freedom of movement, the security of the population and freedom of speech, assembly and the press;

(b) Permit the organization and holding of political meetings, rallies, demonstrations and marches;

(c) Publicize through available and appropriate media the issues regarding the referendum and points of view of the population;

(d) Facilitate the peaceful return to the Territory of all persons eligible to vote in the referendum;

(e) Deal with complaints that the provisions of the settlement proposals, or of the referendum regulations, or the rules or instructions issued pursuant thereto, have not been complied with;

(f) Ensure that law and order is maintained in the Territory for purposes of the referendum process through the monitoring of existing police activities and the deployment of the MINURSO Security (Civil Police) Unit and that no one can resort to intimidation or interfere in the referendum process.

E. Referendum

65. As far as the actual conduct of the referendum is concerned, the Referendum Commission will advise the Special Representative on matters such as:

(a) The date of the referendum;
(b) The requirements for polling stations, ballot boxes and ballot forms;
(c) The manner and conduct of voting;
(d) The association of the official observers from the parties and the representatives of OAU with the voting process;
(e) The tally of the voting and the issuance of the results of the voting;
(f) The lodging of any petitions concerning the results of the voting;
(g) The definition and determination of offences relating to the referendum and their consequences.

66. In the performance of their functions the Identification Commission and the Referendum Commission will prepare any rules or instructions of the nature outlined in paragraph 58 above that are necessary to give effect to their recommendations and which, after approval by the Special Representative, will be issued and put into effect by all concerned.

IX. Other Responsibilities of the Special Representative During the Transitional Period

67. In addition to his direct responsibility for the organization and conduct of the referendum itself, the Special Representative will also be required to satisfy himself that the necessary conditions are otherwise met in order to guarantee the organization of a free and fair referendum. He will accordingly monitor closely the manner in which the authorities involved carry out their day-to-day responsibility for other aspects of the administration of the Territory during the transitional period. If he concludes that any steps or measures would conflict with the agreed objective of holding a free and fair referendum to enable the people of Western Sahara to determine their future without military or administrative constraints, he will bring the matter to the attention of those concerned with a view to an amicable settlement. Should any differences persist the Special Representative will report the matter to the Secretary-General for such action as the Secretary-General may think fit.

68. The Special Representative will pay special attention to the arrangements made for the maintenance of law and order during the transitional period. In this respect, it is envisaged in particular that the Special Representative will have exclusive authority in all United Nations premises connected with the referendum and in their immediate vicinity, such as voter registration offices and polling stations. This authority would include the maintenance of law and order in such premises, the Special Representative being provided with United Nations civil police for this purpose. Such civil police, in cases of emergency, could call upon the Military Unit of MINURSO to

render assistance to them. In other areas, the activities of the existing police forces will be closely monitored by the Security (Civil Police) Unit of MINURSO.

69. Before the beginning of the referendum campaign, the neutralization of the paramilitary units in the existing police forces (the "mobile action companies" and "auxiliary forces") will be carried out through the deposit of their weapons, ammunition and military equipment in armouries where their safe custody will be monitored by the Military Unit of MINURSO.

X. Release of Political Prisoners and Suspension of Laws Which Might Impede a Free and Fair Referendum

70. The Special Representative will take steps with the two parties to ensure the release, before the beginning of the referendum campaign, of all Western Saharan political prisoners or detainees and to this end an amnesty is envisaged as the first stage. In this work he will be assisted by an independent jurist appointed by the Secretary-General. Any difference concerning the release of political prisoners or detainees will be settled in a manner satisfactory to the Special Representative.

71. Before the beginning of the referendum campaign, the Special Representative will ensure that the authorities involved suspend any law or measure which, in his judgement, could obstruct the conduct of a free and fair referendum and which would not otherwise be superseded by the regulations, rules and instructions referred to in paragraph 58 above.

XI. Return of Refugees, Other Western Saharans and Members of Frente POLISARIO Entitled to Vote

72. Following the completion of the work of the Identification Commission, all refugees who have been identified as having the right to vote in the referendum and who have expressed the wish to return to the Territory will be enabled to do so, together with their immediate families, through a programme organized by UNHCR. The Special Representative will designate a number of points at which returnees will be able to cross into the Territory. Security at these crossing-points and at reception centres established by UNHCR will be provided by the Military Unit of MINURSO. The Special Representative will also take such steps as may be necessary to ensure that the returnees will be able to take part in the referendum, without restriction or risk of being arrested, detained, intimidated or imprisoned. To this end they will be granted a general and complete amnesty.

73. Likewise, other Western Saharans, not refugees but resident outside the Territory, who are found eligible to vote by the Identification Commission, will be permitted to return to the Territory, together with their immediate families. It is the Secretary-General's intention to ask the High Commissioner for

Refugees to extend his good offices to these Western Saharans and to assume responsibility for their voluntary repatriation from designated locations in neighbouring countries.

74. Frente POLISARIO combatants found eligible to vote who wish to take part in the referendum will be enabled to return, peacefully and without arms or uniforms, together with their immediate families, in accordance with the arrangements described in the two preceding paragraphs, including the amnesty. The arms, ammunition and military equipment of returning Frente POLISARIO combatants will be deposited at the locations referred to in paragraph 57 above where their safe custody will be monitored by the Military Unit of MINURSO. The disposition of these arms, ammunition and equipment will be decided after the results of the referendum are known.

XII. Proclamation of the Referendum Results

75. The results of the referendum shall be proclaimed as indicated in paragraph 47 (j) above. If the decision is for independence, the withdrawal of all remaining Moroccan troops will begin within 24 hours and will be completed within 6 weeks. The withdrawal will be monitored by the Military Unit of MINURSO. If the decision is for integration with Morocco, the demobilization of any Frente POLISARIO troops who have not returned to take part in the referendum will begin within 24 hours of the proclamation of the result and will be completed within 4 weeks, under the monitoring of the Military Unit of MINURSO.

76. As soon as the results of the referendum have been proclaimed, the Special Representative will begin to reduce United Nations personnel in Western Sahara. The Special Representative and his remaining civilian and military staff will complete their withdrawal as soon as possible after all the tasks assigned to them by the Security Council have been satisfactorily carried out.

XIII. Composition and Tasks of the United Nations Mission for the Referendum in Western Sahara

77. The Secretary-General has defined the tasks of the three units (civilian, military and security) that are provided for in the settlement proposals, and which will make up MINURSO, in the light of the responsibilities of the United Nations described above.

A. Civilian unit

78. The Civilian Unit, which is central to the operation, will comprise the office of the Special Representative and his support staff in fields such as administration, legal and legislative matters, questions relating to refugees and political detainees, information and public relations. In addition, a major

part of the Civilian Unit will be responsible for the organization and conduct of the referendum. The Unit will consist largely of officials of the United Nations. It is hoped, however, that a significant number of personnel, especially personnel directly concerned with the organization and conduct of the referendum, will be made available by Governments at the Secretary-General's request.

B. Security unit

79. The Security Unit will be made up of civil police. Their task will be:

(a) To ensure tranquillity and maintain law and order in the vicinity of, and at, voter registration offices and polling stations, to ensure that no person is denied entry for the purposes of registration or voting and, when specifically so ordered, to maintain order at other locations where activities in connection with the referendum, under MINURSO auspices or authority, are taking place;

(b) To monitor the activities of the existing police forces so as to ensure that they are acting in strict accordance with the settlement proposals and the present implementation plan, which are intended to secure the organization of a free and fair referendum without military or administrative constraints and to prevent any possibility of intimidation or interference from any quarter.

80. The Security Unit will be commanded by a Police Commissioner appointed by the Secretary-General. The members of the Unit will be provided by Governments, at the request of the Secretary-General. Its terms of reference, which will be drawn up on the authority of the Secretary-General, will define the circumstances under which members of the Civil Police Unit may in the course of their duties take offenders into custody, and the procedures to be followed thereafter. The terms of reference will also spell out the monitoring responsibility of members of the Security Unit and the procedures they are to follow in submitting the details of any infractions involved to the Special Representative for action.

C. Military unit

81. The tasks of the Military Unit will be:

(a) To monitor the cease-fire;
(b) To verify the agreed reduction in troops;
(c) To monitor the confinement of troops of both sides to agreed locations;
(d) To monitor the custody of certain arms and ammunition;

(e) To provide security for the return of Western Saharans from outside the Territory at designated crossing-points and at UNHCR
reception centres;

(f) To assist the Security Unit, as required;

(g) Depending on the results of the referendum, to monitor the
activities described in paragraph 75 above.

82. To perform the above tasks the Military Unit will require military
observers, infantry, an air unit and other logistics personnel. It will be under
the command of the United Nations, vested in the Secretary-General, under
the authority of the Security Council. The command in the field will be
exercised by a force commander appointed by the Secretary-General after
consultation with the parties and with the consent of the Security Council.
The Force Commander will report to the Secretary-General through the
Special Representative. The normal rules in United Nations peace-keeping
operations for the bearing and use of arms will apply. The Secretary-
General will report regularly to the Security Council on the functioning of
the Military Unit, as on the other activities of MINURSO. The military personnel of MINURSO will be contributed by States Members of the United
Nations, at the request of the Secretary-General, who will consult the parties and obtain the Security Council's approval of the composition of the
Military Unit.

XIV. Observations

83. The present report is presented to the Security Council in pursuance
of paragraph 2 of resolution 621 (1988) in which the Security Council
requested the Secretary-General to transmit to it as soon as possible a report
on the holding of a referendum for self-determination of the people of
Western Sahara and on ways and means to ensure the organization and conduct of such a referendum by the United Nations in co-operation with
OAU. I believe that the implementation plan contained in the present report
provides an effective means of holding such a referendum and permitting
the people of Western Sahara to determine their future without military or
administrative constraints. I accordingly commend it to the Security Council for such action as the Council may think appropriate in order to facilitate its implementation at the earliest possible date.

84. It will be clear from the present report that the United Nations
operation in Western Sahara will be large and complicated. There are at
present unknown factors and it is not possible at this stage to present to the
Council even a preliminary estimate of what the cost will be. It is therefore
my intention to dispatch, in the immediate future, a technical mission to the
Territory and to neighbouring countries to refine the administrative aspects

of the plan outlined in the present report and to obtain the information, especially information about the availability of logistic supplies and support in the Territory, which is required to prepare a further report to the Security Council containing an estimate of the cost of MINURSO, and, in due course, a detailed budget for submission to the General Assembly.

85. It will be my intention, when submitting the further report to the Security Council, to recommend that it authorize the immediate establishment of MINURSO for purposes described in the present report. At the same time, I shall recommend that, if the Council decides to set up MINURSO, its costs should be considered as expenses of the Organization to be borne by the Member States in accordance with Article 17, paragraph 2, of the Charter. I would intend to recommend to the General Assembly that the assessments to be levied on Member States be credited to a special account that would be established for this purpose.

Appendix 2

Security Council Resolution 658 (1990)

The Situation Concerning Western Sahara[1]

Decision

At its 2929th meeting, on 27 June 1990, the Council discussed the item entitled "The situation concerning Western Sahara: report of the Secretary-General (S/21360)."[2]

Resolution 658 (1990) of 27 June 1990

The Security Council,

Recalling its resolution 621 (1988) of 20 September 1988, by which it decided to authorize the Secretary-General to appoint a special representative for Western Sahara and to request the Secretary-General to transmit to it as soon as possible a report on the holding of a referendum for self-determination of the people of Western Sahara and on ways and means to ensure the organization and supervision of such a referendum by the United Nations in co-operation with the Organization of African Unity,

Recalling also that, on 30 August 1988, the Kingdom of Morocco and the Frente Popular para la Liberación de Saguía el-Hamra y de Río de Oro gave their agreement in principle to the proposals of the Secretary-General of the United Nations and the current Chairman of the Assembly of Heads of State and Government of the Organization of African Unity in the framework of their joint mission of good offices,

Having considered the report of the Secretary-General on the situation concerning Western Sahara,[3]

1. *Expresses* its full support to the Secretary-General in his mission of good offices, pursued jointly with the current Chairman of the Assembly of Heads of State and Government of the Organization of African Unity, with a view to settling the question of Western Sahara;

2. *Approves* the report of the Secretary-General,[4] transmitted to the Council in accordance with resolution 621 (1988) with a view to settling the question of Western Sahara, which contains the full text of the settlement proposals as accepted by the two parties on 30 August 1988 as well as an outline of the plan provided by the Secretary-General in order to implement those proposals;

3. *Calls upon* the two parties to co-operate fully with the Secretary-General of the United Nations and the current Chairman of the Assembly of Heads of State and Government of the Organization of African Unity in their efforts aimed at an early settlement of the question of Western Sahara;

4. *Welcomes* the intention of the Secretary-General to dispatch, in the immediate future, a technical mission to the territory and to neighbouring countries, in particular to refine the administrative aspects of the outlined plan and to obtain the necessary information for the preparation of a further report to the Council;

5. *Requests* the Secretary-General to transmit to the Security Council as soon as possible a further detailed report on his implementation plan, containing, in particular, an estimate of the cost of the United Nations Mission for the referendum in Western Sahara, on the understanding that this further report should be the basis on which the Council would authorize the establishment of the Mission.

Adopted unanimously at the 2929th meeting.

Notes

1. Resolutions or decisions on this question were also adopted by the Council in 1975 and 1988.

2. See *Official Records of the Security Council, Forty-fifth Year, Supplement for April, May and June 1990.*

3. *Ibid.,* document S/21360.

4. *Ibid.*

Appendix 3

Identification and Registration of Voters: Excerpt from Report of the Secretary-General S/22464 of 19 April 1991

Identification and Registration of Voters

19. A central element in the settlement proposals is the identification and registration of all Western Saharans eligible to vote in the referendum. This work will be entrusted to the Identification Commission. It is stated in the settlement proposals (S/21360, para. 25) that "the Commission will perform its task during the transitional period." It has, however, become clear that, as explained below, certain tasks can, and indeed must, be completed outside and inside the Territory before the cease-fire comes into effect. I accordingly intend to appoint the members of the Identification Commission as soon as the Security Council has decided to establish MINURSO, so that, under the direction of my Special Representative, they can begin the necessary preparatory work without delay, beginning with the establishment of the Commission's rules of procedure.

20. The Identification Commission's task will be to implement the proposals, agreed upon by the two parties, that all Western Saharans to whom the 1974 census undertaken by the Spanish authorities related and who are aged 18 years or over will have the right to vote, whether they are currently present in the Territory or living outside it as refugees or for other reasons. The Commission's mandate to update the 1974 census will include (a) removing from the lists the names of persons who have since died and (b) considering applications from persons who claim the right to participate in the referendum on the grounds that they are Western Saharans and were omitted from the 1974 census. The tribal chiefs of Western Sahara will be asked to contribute to the Identification Commission's work. A preliminary meeting took place with a representative group of tribal chiefs at Geneva in June 1990. Further discussions with tribal chiefs will be held, after the decision has been taken to establish MINURSO, in order to refine the Commission's operational procedures. The parties and representatives of OAU will,

as appropriate, participate as official observers in the work of the Identification Commission.

21. The first stage of the Commission's work will be to update the 1974 census list. As a preparatory step, a copy of this list was transmitted to each of the parties on 16 October 1990, with a request for any available information about persons who have died since 1974 and about the whereabouts of those who remain alive, whether inside or outside the Territory. Both of the parties have been asked to provide this information soon. Its early receipt will facilitate the Identification Commission's work, which is to commence immediately after the General Assembly has approved MINURSO's budget. The Commission, having made much revisions to the 1974 list as seem to it appropriate, will arrange for the revised list to be published in the Territory and in places outside where numbers of Western Saharans are known to be living. At the same time, the Commission will publish instructions on how individual Western Saharans can apply in writing, before a specified date, for inclusion in the list on the grounds that they were omitted from the 1974 census. It is estimated that four weeks will be required for this part of the Commission's work. A further period of four weeks will be set for the Commission to receive individual written applications for the inclusion of names in the list. The applications will be classified and the Commission, assisted by the tribal chiefs and in the presence of observers from OAU and the parties, will meet in New York or Geneva to review them under the supervision of the Special Representative. It is estimated that this review will take up to four weeks. When it has been completed and prior to D-Day, a consolidated list of the names of persons who, on the basis of the revised 1974 census and the review of applications received, have been judged to be eligible to vote will, with my clearance, be published in the Territory and in places outside where numbers of Saharans are known to be living.

22. By D-Day the Identification Commission will be fully established in the mission area. The Commission will be assisted in its work by the field offices established at principal population centres as well as by static and mobile teams, consisting of a leader, three identification/registration officers, a clerk/typist, two civilian police monitors and support staff such as interpreters and drivers.

23. At this second stage in its work, the Commission will undertake two main functions, in each of which it will be assisted by the tribal chiefs. The functions will be:

(a) To identify, and issue registration cards to, persons whose names are on the published list of eligible voters;
(b) To provide, and organize procedures, for appeals against non-inclusion of names in the published list or against decisions made under subparagraph (a) above.

Arrangements will be made for the Commission to identify and register, at the designated locations, all Frente POLISARIO troops who are eligible to vote, as well as any Western Saharans who are similarly eligible and may be serving in the Moroccan forces.

24. It is envisaged that a period of up to 11 weeks will be required for this second stage of the Commission's work. When it has been completed, the Special Representative will submit to me, for consideration in consultation with the current Chairman of OAU, a consolidated list of all registered voters. The final voters list will be published as soon as it has been authorized by me.

Appendix 4

Instructions Relating to the Tasks of the Indentification Commission*: Annex to Report of the Secretary-General S/23299 of 19 December 1991

I. Preliminary Remarks

1. In conformity with paragraph 58 of document S/21360 and paragraph 9 of document S/22464, as well as chapter 3 of the general regulations issued by the Secretary-General on 8 November 1991, the following instructions regarding the process of identification of Saharans eligible to participate in the referendum are hereby enunciated.

2. It should be recalled that, according to the settlement plan, four essential conditions must be met to achieve the goal of holding a free, fair and impartial referendum for the Western Saharan population and to enable the United Nations Mission for the Referendum in Western Sahara (MINURSO) to carry out its responsibilities effectively and impartially: support and backing of the Security Council; full cooperation of the two parties; cooperation and support of the neighbouring countries; and the necessary financial resources.[1]

II. Provisions of the Plan Regarding Identification

3. Under the provisions of the plan, the Secretary-General is to set up, in consultation with the current Chairman of the Organization of African Unity (OAU), an identification commission responsible for carefully and scrupulously reviewing the 1974 census and updating it.[2] The plan also provides that the role of the Identification Commission will be:

(a) To review carefully the census taken in the Territory in 1974 by the Spanish authorities and update it;

(b) To calculate the real growth of the Saharan population in the period between the date of the above census and the date of organization of the referendum, taking into account the following elements:

(i) births and deaths;
(ii) movements of the Saharan population.[3]

4. On the basis of the information mentioned above, the Identification Commission will establish as precisely as possible the number of Saharans living in the Territory of Western Sahara and the number of Saharan refugees and non-residents qualified to participate in the referendum.[4]

5. In respect of the identification and registration of voters, the plan provides that, under the terms of the settlement proposals, the Identification Commission will implement the agreed position of the parties that all Western Saharans counted in the 1974 census undertaken by the Spanish authorities and aged 18 or over will have the right to vote, whether currently present in the Territory or outside as refugees or for other reasons.[5]

6. In its resolution 658 (1990) of 27 June 1990, the Security Council, *inter alia,* requested the Secretary-General to transmit to the Security Council a further detailed report, on the understanding that the further report should be the basis on which the Security Council would authorize the establishment of MINURSO (see para. 5 of resolution 658 (1990)). In paragraph 2 of his report, the Secretary-General confirmed that he had addressed the main elements of the implementation plan and added details that might be of assistance to members of the Security Council in their consideration of the recommendation regarding the establishment of MINURSO.

7. In this context, document S/22464 provides that the Identification Commission's mandate to update the 1974 census will include (a) removing from the lists the names of persons who have since died and (b) considering applications from persons who claim the right to participate in the referendum on the grounds that they are Western Saharans and were omitted from the 1974 census. It is also provided that the United Nations will ask the tribal chiefs of Western Sahara to contribute to the Identification Commission's work.[6]

8. As noted in paragraph 19 of the same document, the identification and registration of all Western Saharans eligible to vote in the referendum constitute a central element in the settlement proposals. They represent also one of the most difficult tasks, as was underlined by the United Nations Visiting Mission as early as 1975, when it observed that problems would arise in determining eligibility to participate in a referendum.[7]

III. Specific Aspects of the Saharan Society

9. The difficulties of the identification process are due, in particular, to the characteristics of the Western Saharan population, notably its nomadic

tradition and the tribal structure of the society. In that respect, the above-mentioned report observed: "because of their nomadic way of life, the people of the Territory move easily across the borders to the neigbouring [*sic*] countries, where they are received by members of their tribes or even of their families. This ebb and flow of people across the borders of the Territory makes it difficult to take a complete census of the inhabitants of Spanish Sahara and also poses the complex problem of the identification of the Saharans of the Territory and makes it even more difficult to take a satisfactory census of refugees."[8]

10. The Saharan society remains for the most part a society structured around tribal membership, each tribe being subdivided in fractions, subfractions, and family groups (*ahels*). Some of these tribes extend beyond the borders of Western Sahara. Under the heading "status of an indigenous inhabitant," the 1975 report observed that "in view of the close affinity which exists between Saharans living within the Territory and those in neighbouring countries and also of their nomadic tradition, the question of determining who is and who is not an indigenous inhabitant of the Territory is a somewhat complex matter."[9] That complexity notwithstanding, it is clear that only members of tribes whose connection with the Territory within the limits of recognized international borders is clearly established should participate in the referendum.

11. To the difficulties related to the Saharan way of life and the structure of the society, one must add those resulting from conflicts that took place in the Territory over several decades, leading a large number of Saharans to seek refuge, at different times, in neighbouring countries. In addition, other Saharans indigenous to the Territory had to leave it for economic reasons, whether to migrate as a result of drought or to seek employment in neighbouring countries.

12. In view of the above, it is clear that a comprehensive count of indigenous Saharans, including those absent from the Territory, is a complex task. It should be recalled that, according to the Spanish authorities and the representatives of Saharan political movements met in 1975 by the United Nations visiting mission, any census of indigenous persons undertaken outside the Territory would have to be based on proven membership of social and family groups (fractions and subfractions of tribes) existing within the Territory.[10]

IV. Specific Aspects of the 1974 Census

13. Notwithstanding the difficulties noted above, the identification of the Saharan population living in Western Sahara was undertaken by the Spanish colonial administration. In particular, it carried out in 1974 a population census, which is referred to in the settlement plan. At the end of this

census, the total count of Saharans living in the Territory was 73,497. In addition, as part of its identification effort, the colonial administration issued, between 1970 and 1976, a total of 32,516 national identity documents.

14. Those national identity documents, which were the basis for the census exercise, were issued by a permanent commission composed of tribal chiefs. The criteria for determining whether or not a Saharan was indigenous to the Territory was membership in a family group (*ahel*) which existed in the Territory. It was pointed out to the United Nations visiting mission that "all the members of such groups are known to each other and that the authenticity of a claim to belong to a family group can be verified by the sheiks and notables of that group in consultation with their members."[11]

15. It is recognized by the parties and the tribal chiefs that the 1974 census did not include all the Saharans from the Territory. On the one hand, a number of Saharans present in the Territory, whether or not they possessed a national identity document, were not contacted by the census teams, and, on the other hand, part of the population of the Territory lived, and still lives, outside Western Sahara, for a variety of reasons. It should be recalled that, in its final communiqué, the meeting of tribal chiefs organized by the United Nations in June 1990 recognized "the imperfections and inadequacies" of the 1974 census, and "among other things the fact that many Saharans and Saharan refugees were omitted."

16. In order to carry out the role entrusted to it, the Identification Commission must review the cases of Saharans indigenous to Western Sahara who, at the time of the census, either were present in the Territory but were not counted, or were absent from the Territory, notably for the reasons mentioned in paragraph 11 above. To ensure that all eligible Saharans are given an opportunity to participate in the referendum on the future status of the Territory, the Identification Commission must, with complete impartiality, make use of all resources and expertise at its disposal, particularly the tribal chiefs and notables.

V. Role of the Tribal Chiefs and Notables

17. In view of the above-mentioned characteristics of the Saharan society, one can hardly overemphasize the crucial role of the cooperation and assistance of tribal chiefs and other notables of the Territory. Their contribution is indispensable at all stages of the identification process: to assist the Commission in refining its operational procedures;[12] to assist in the review of the written applications from people who were not counted during the 1974 census;[13] and to assist in identifying and registering voters, and in connection with the process of appeals.[14]

18. With their assistance, the Commission will review applications, taking into account relevant circumstances, in an impartial and just manner, with respect to all Saharans eligible to participate in the referendum.

VI. Cooperation of the Parties

19. Such a complex exercise can succeed only with the cooperation of the parties in a spirit of objectivity and fairness. To carry out its task, the Commission must work in an atmosphere of trust and serenity which the parties must promote. Needless to say that without their cooperation, even the most vigorous efforts by the United Nations cannot enable it to fulfil its mission, whatever the human resources and financial means put at its disposal.

VII. Instructions for the Review of Applications for Participation in the Referendum

20. Taking into account all the preceding considerations, these instructions have been developed for the guidance of the Identification Commission. They take into account recognized sources such as custom, international practice, generally recognized norms as well as laws in force in the region.

21. In applying them, the Commission will bear in mind, above all, that, for actual identification, it is the membership of a family group (subfraction of a tribe) existing within the Territory, which can be attested to by the sheiks and notables of the family group, that should eventually prevail for eligibility to participate in the referendum.

22. These guidelines apply to Saharans aged 18 years or more at the closing date for inclusion in the voters' list and are drawn directly from the provisions of the plan. They must be applied by the Identification Commission, in the light of the preceding paragraph and of all available information and relevant circumstances. This can be achieved only with the assistance of tribal chiefs and the support of the parties.

23. It is understood that persons whose names are included in the revised 1974 census list are eligible to participate in the referendum. It is also understood that members of the immediate family (father, mother and children) of Saharans whose name is included in the original census list or in the revised census list will, owing to this close relationship, be allowed to participate in the referendum. The relationship will be established on the basis of an individual application.

24. With regard to other applications from people who claim the right to participate in the referendum on the ground that they are Saharans and

were not counted during the 1974 census, the Commission must be mindful of several considerations stemming from a concern for justice and fairness.

25. It is understood that, upon presentation of an individual application, persons who lived in the Territory as members of a Saharan tribe at the time of the 1974 census and could not be counted are eligible to vote on the same ground as people who were counted. Testimonies or documents must be submitted in support of all individual applications.

26. In order to align the treatment granted to Saharans present but not counted at the time of the 1974 census to that of people whose name is on the census list, members of the immediate family of the former group (father, mother and children) are equally eligible to vote.

27. In respect of those members of a Saharan tribe indigenous to the Territory who, for the reasons mentioned in section IV above, were absent from Western Sahara at the time of the census, it is considered that their absence from the Territory at that time cannot justify that they be automatically deprived of their right to participate in the decision regarding the future of Western Sahara.

28. It is necessary, however, that the link with the Territory of people absent in 1974 be solid and demonstrable. To develop guidelines in that respect, the United Nations has taken into account the concerns of the parties as well as the customs of the Saharan society. For instance, it should be recalled that in 1974 the *yema'a,* comprising Saharan traditional authorities, adopted norms for the issuance of identity documents to Saharans.[15] To the extent appropriate, these norms were also taken into consideration.

29. Firstly, it is considered that an appropriate link to the Territory exists when the applicant was born of a Saharan father born in the Territory. In that regard, consideration was given to the fact that, in 1974, Saharan tribal chiefs themselves developed a liberal norm, patterned after their own tradition. It is also appropriate to note that one of the main tasks of the United Nations has been to promote decolonization around the world. In that context, people who fled colonial rule cannot be deprived of the right to decide on the future of the Territory to which they belong. Similarly, children, aged 18 years or more, should not be penalized just because their parents, owing to colonialism or other reasons mentioned above, chose or were obliged to leave their homes. However, in order not to widen excessively the scope of this provision, it has been restricted to one generation only.

30. Secondly, taking into account current provisions regulating the acquisition of nationality in the countries of the region, it is considered that a member of a Saharan tribe belonging to the Territory is eligible to participate in the referendum if he or she has resided in the Territory for a period of six consecutive years before 1 December 1974. That figure is not arbitrary: the period of six consecutive years represents the average period of

residence required under the legal systems of the countries of the region as a condition for the acquisition of nationality.

31. Lastly, as an uninterrupted period of six years might penalize those Saharans who, owing to a variety of circumstances, have had to move frequently across the borders of the Territory, it was considered necessary to provide for a condition of an intermittent residence period of 12 years prior to 1 December 1974.

VIII. Conclusions

32. The process of identification of people eligible to participate in the referendum will involve a number of proofs that applicants will have to provide in support of their claim. Official documents, well known to the Saharans and used by them, will help the Commission in making its assessment. In addition, the Commission will take into consideration the fact that in the Saharan society, oral testimonies play an important part in all social activities. Those testimonies, given under appropriate conditions, will also assist the Commission in judging the merits of individual applications.

33. The United Nations is well aware that such a complex task as the identification of the Saharans cannot be accomplished hastily. In this regard, It is appropriate to recall the settlement plan, which states: "eligibility to vote will depend either on the presence of a person's name in the 1974 census list or on a person's ability to convince the Identification Commission that he or she is a Western Saharan who was omitted from the 1974 census. Matching individuals with names in a 17-year-old list is bound to take time. In a society that is nomadic and to a large extent illiterate and where such criteria as place of birth or residence are of limited relevance, the adjudication of applications from persons claiming to have been omitted from the 1974 list will also be time consuming. If the referendum is to be fair and impartial, in accordance with the settlement proposals, these processes cannot be rushed."[16]

34. Furthermore, this process of identification can be carried out only with the complete cooperation of the parties, in a spirit of justice and objectivity. Without such cooperation and without equity and justice on the part of all concerned, particularly the tribal chiefs, the notables and the members of the *ahels,* the guidelines cannot, by themselves alone, enable the United Nations to fulfil in a satisfactory manner the task entrusted to it.

Notes

*In accordance with chapter 3 of the general regulations promulgated by the Secretary-General on 8 November 1991. Further instructions relating to the tasks of the Commission, including its procedures and method of work, will be issued later, as required.

1. S/22464, para. 55.
2. S/21360, para. 25.
3. Ibid., para. 27.
4. Ibid., para. 28.
5. Ibid., para. 61.
6. S/22464, para. 20.
7. A/10023/Rev.l, annex, para. 157.
8. Ibid., para. 11.
9. Ibid., annex. para. 155.
10. Ibid., para. 125.
11. Ibid., para. 158.
12. S/22464, para. 20.
13. Ibid., para. 21.
14. Ibid., para. 23.
15. According to the first norm, shall be deemed Saharans "all persons born of Saharan father." See document A/10023/Rev.l, annex, para. 160.
16. S/22464, op. cit., para. 62, subpara. (a).

Appendix 5

Peace Plan for Self-Determination of the People of Western Sahara: Annex II to Report of the Secretary-General S/2003/565 of 23 May 2003

I. Purpose

1. The present peace plan for self-determination of the people of Western Sahara is an agreement by and between the Kingdom of Morocco and the Frente POLISARIO (which are the interested parties), joined by the People's Democratic Republic of Algeria and the Islamic Republic of Mauritania (which are the neighbouring countries) and the United Nations. The purpose of the plan is to achieve a political solution to the conflict in Western Sahara that provides for self-determination, as contemplated in paragraph 1 of Security Council resolution 1429 (2002), of 30 July 2002. The effective date of the plan is the date when all interested parties, neighbouring countries and the United Nations have signed it. The final status of Western Sahara shall be determined by a referendum conducted in accordance with part II of the plan. During the period between the effective date of the plan and the implementation of the results of the referendum on final status, governmental authority shall be exercised in Western Sahara in accordance with part III of the plan.

II. Self-Determination Referendum

2. A referendum to determine the final status of Western Sahara shall be held no earlier than four and no later than five years after the effective date of the plan. The options or ballot questions to be included in the referendum will include: (a) those previously agreed to in the settlement plan; and (b) any additional options or ballot questions agreed to by the Kingdom of Morocco and the Western Sahara Authority (as defined in para. 8 (a) below).

3. A referendum option or ballot question shall be deemed to have been adopted if it receives more than 50 per cent of the votes cast in the referendum. If more than two options or ballot questions are presented and none

receives a majority of the votes cast in the first round, a second round shall be held in which the two options or ballot questions that received the most votes shall be presented to the voters.

4. The referendum shall be organized and conducted by the United Nations and monitored by international observers accredited by the United Nations.

5. Those eligible to vote in the referendum are those persons who are at least 18 years of age and: (a) who have been identified as qualified to vote by the Identification Commission of the United Nations Mission for the Referendum in Western Sahara (MINURSO), as reflected on the provisional voter list of 30 December 1999 (without giving effect to any appeals or other objections); (b) whose names appear on the repatriation list drawn up by the United Nations High Commissioner for Refugees (UNHCR) as at 31 October 2000; or (c) who have resided continuously in Western Sahara since 30 December 1999. Those eligible to vote shall be determined by the United Nations, whose decision shall be final and without appeal.

6. The addition to the list of qualified voters of any person whose name does not appear either on the provisional voter list of 30 December 1999 or on the repatriation list drawn up by UNHCR as at 31 October 2000 can occur only if the status of that person as a continuous resident of Western Sahara since 30 December 1999 is supported by testimony from at least three credible persons and/or credible documentary evidence. The United Nations shall: (a) determine the credibility and legal sufficiency of all such testimony and other evidence; and (b) based on that testimony and other evidence, determine who is (and is not) entitled to be added to the list of qualified voters under this paragraph. These determinations by the United Nations shall be final and without appeal.

7. All interested parties and neighbouring countries agree to accept and respect the results of the referendum.

III. Authority in Western Sahara

8. Governmental authority in Western Sahara between the effective date of this plan and such time as a new government shall take office in implementation of the result of the referendum on final status shall be as set forth in this plan, and in particular in the present paragraph:

> (a) The population of Western Sahara, acting through the executive, legislative and judicial bodies established under the plan—herein sometimes referred to as the Western Sahara Authority—shall be responsible for and have exclusive competence over local government, the territorial budget, taxation, economic development, internal security, law enforcement, social welfare,

cultural affairs, education, commerce, transportation, agriculture, mining, fisheries, industry, environment, housing and urban development, water and electricity, roads and other basic infrastructure;

(b) Morocco shall be responsible for and have exclusive competence over foreign relations (including international agreements and conventions), national security and external defence (including the determination of borders—maritime, aerial, and terrestrial—and their protection by all appropriate means), all matters relating to the production, sale, ownership and use of weapons and explosives (except for the duly authorized use of weapons by the law enforcement authorities of the Western Sahara Authority) and the preservation of territorial integrity against secessionist attempts, whether from within or outside the Territory, provided, however, that the right to preserve territorial integrity shall not authorize any action whatsoever that would prevent, suppress, or stifle peaceful public debate, discourse or campaign activity, particularly during any election or referendum period. In addition, the flag, currency, customs, postal and telecommunication systems of Morocco shall be the same for Western Sahara. With respect to all functions described in this subparagraph, Morocco may appoint representatives to serve it in Western Sahara.

9. The authority of Morocco for the foreign relations of Western Sahara shall be exercised in consultation with the Western Sahara Authority on matters that directly affect the interests of Western Sahara. Morocco may authorize representatives of the Authority to serve as members of the Kingdom's diplomatic delegations in international meetings concerned with economic issues and other issues of direct interest to Western Sahara.

10. The executive authority of the Western Sahara Authority shall be exercised by a Chief Executive elected by the people of Western Sahara in accordance with paragraphs 15 to 17 of the present plan. The Chief Executive may appoint such administrators as may be necessary to exercise the powers reserved to the Authority by the plan.

11. The legislative authority of the Western Sahara Authority shall be exercised by a Legislative Assembly elected by the people of Western Sahara in accordance with paragraphs 15 to 17 of the present plan. The Legislative Assembly shall be responsible for the enactment of all laws applicable in Western Sahara, with the exception of any relating to the authorities reserved to Morocco under paragraph 8 (b) above.

12. The judicial authority in Western Sahara shall be vested in a Supreme Court of Western Sahara and such other lower courts as may be established by the Western Sahara Authority. Members of the Supreme Court and lower courts shall be appointed by the Chief Executive, with the consent of the Legislative Assembly. The Supreme Court (a) shall have jurisdiction to

adjudicate the compatibility of any law of Western Sahara with this plan (except any relating to the authorities reserved to Morocco by paragraph 8 (b) above, in which case the highest court of Morocco shall have that juris-diction), and (b) shall be the final authority in interpreting the law of West-ern Sahara. The Supreme Court shall have the authority to declare null and void any law, regulation or other act of the Western Sahara Authority that contravenes this plan or exceeds the competence of the Authority, as pro-vided in the plan.

13. All laws, regulations and acts of the Western Sahara Authority shall be consistent with internationally recognized human rights standards (including human rights standards in any treaties to which Morocco is a party). In no event shall human rights in Western Sahara be protected to a lesser extent than is provided for in the constitution and laws of Morocco.

14. All laws and regulations now in force in Western Sahara shall con-tinue in force until they are amended or repealed by action of the Legisla-tive Assembly and Chief Executive of the Western Sahara Authority, except any relating to the authorities reserved to Morocco by paragraph 8 (b) above.

15. The election for the Legislative Assembly and Chief Executive of the Western Sahara Authority shall be held within one year of the effective date of this plan. Voters shall vote separately (in a single election) for the Chief Executive and members of the Legislative Assembly, who shall hold office for a period of four years or until governmental authority in Western Sahara is changed pursuant to the final status referendum. Sole and exclu-sive authority over all matters relating to any and all elections and referen-dums called for in this plan, including their organization and conduct, shall be vested in the United Nations.

16. Those eligible to vote in the election for the Legislative Assembly and Chief Executive of the Western Sahara Authority are persons who are at least 18 years of age and whose names appear either on the provisional voter list of 30 December 1999 (without giving effect to any appeals or other objections) or on the repatriation list drawn up by UNHCR as at 31 October 2000. Those eligible to vote shall be determined by the United Nations, whose decision shall be final and without appeal.

IV. Other Matters

17. Campaigns for the election and referendum referred to in this plan shall be conducted in a manner consistent with international human rights standards and in keeping with the principles of the Code of Conduct agreed to by Morocco and the Frente POLISARIO in 1997 (the Houston accords), except where to do so would be inconsistent with this plan. In particular,

the interested parties agree not to hinder the ability of persons to campaign peacefully for or against any person standing for election or any option or ballot question offered to the voters in the referendum on final status.

18. Neither Morocco nor the Western Sahara Authority may unilaterally change or abolish the status of Western Sahara, except for the adoption of such laws as may be necessary to conform to the results of the referendum on final status. No change to this plan may be made without the agreement of the King of Morocco and the Chief Executive and the Legislative Assembly of Western Sahara.

19. Immediately after the effective date of this plan, all political prisoners and prisoners of war shall be released, and the obligation of each party in this regard is not dependent upon performance by the other. The interested parties agree that they shall continue their full cooperation with relevant international bodies until the completion of the repatriation process.

20. Within 90 days after the effective date of this plan, the armed forces of Morocco and the Frente POLISARIO will be reduced, confined, contained and thereafter maintained in all respects strictly in accordance with the provisions of the 1997 Houston accords. This provision is without prejudice to the deployment of Moroccan armed forces in purely defensive positions pursuant to the responsibility of Morocco for external defence under paragraph 8 (b) above or the creation and normal functioning of law enforcement personnel in Western Sahara under the authority of the Western Sahara Authority.

21. The United Nations will assist the interested parties, in particular the Western Sahara Authority, in fulfilling their responsibilities under this plan. The Security Council undertakes to amend the name and mandate of MINURSO to enable it to assist in the implementation of this plan, in particular during the period between the plan's entry into force and the holding of the election for the Chief Executive and the Legislative Assembly of the Western Sahara Authority.

22. The Secretary-General will use his good offices to assist the interested parties in the implementation of this plan. The interested parties agree that the Secretary-General shall have the authority to interpret this plan and that in the event of any disagreement about the meaning of the plan, the Secretary-General's interpretation shall be binding on the interested parties.

Acronyms

AMU	Arab Maghreb Union
AU	African Union (formerly OAU, see below)
FAR	Morocco's Royal Armed Forces
ICJ	International Court of Justice
MINURSO	United Nations Mission for the Referendum in Western Sahara
MOREHOB	Mouvement de Resistance "Les Hommes Bleus"
NATO	North Atlantic Treaty Organization
OAU	Organization of African Unity, now the African Union
Polisario	Frente Popular para la Liberacion de Seguia el-Hamra y Rio de Oro
PUNS	Partido de la Union Nacional Saharaui
RASD	French acronym for SADR, see below
SADR	Sahrawi Arab Democratic Republic
UN	United Nations
UNHCR	United Nations High Commissioner for Refugees

Selected Bibliography

Adebajo, Adekeye. "Selling out the Sahara: The Tragic Tale of the UN Referendum." *Institute for African Development,* Occasional Papers Series, Spring 2002.

Albright, Madeleine. *Madam Secretary.* Macmillan, London, 2003.

Balta, Paul. *Le Grand Maghreb: Des indépendances à l'an 2000.* Paris: La Découverte, 1990.

Barbier, Maurice. *Le conflit du Sahara Occidental.* Paris: L'Harmattan, 1982.

Berramdane, Abdelkhaleq. *Le Sahara Occidental: Enjeu maghrebin.* Paris: Karthala, 1992.

Bolton, John. "Resolving the Western Sahara Conflict." Defense Forum Foundation, Congressional Defense and Foreign Policy Forum, Washington, D.C., 1998 (transcript).

Boutros-Ghali, Boutros. *Unvanquished: A U.S.-U.N. Saga.* New York: Random House, 1999.

Chopra, Jarat. "United Nations Determination of the Western Saharan Self." *Peacekeeping and Multinational Operations* (Norsk Utenrikspolitisk Institut, Oslo), no. 1, March 1994.

———. "A Chance for Peace in Western Sahara." *Survival* 39, no. 3 (Autumn 1997).

Damis, John. *Conflict in Northwest Africa: The Western Sahara Dispute.* Stanford, Calif.: Hoover Institution Press, 1983.

Dunbar, Charles. "Saharan Stasis: Status and Future Prospects of the Western Sahara Conflict." *Middle East Journal* 4 (Fall 2000).

Durch, William J. "Building on Sand: UN Peacekeeping in the Western Sahara." *International Security* 17, no 4 (Spring 1993).

———. "United Nations Mission for the Referendum in Western Sahara." In *The Evolution of UN Peacekeeping.* New York: St. Martin's, 1993.

Fessard de Foucault, Bertrand. "La question du Sahara espagnol." *Revue Francaise d'Etudes Politiques Africaines,* year 10, no. 119 (November 1975).

Franck, Thomas M. "The Stealing of the Sahara." *American Journal of International Law* 70, no. 4 (October 1976).

Froberville, Martine de. *Sahara Occidental: La confiance perdue.* Paris: L'Harmattan, 1996.

Gaudio, Attilio. *Les populations du Sahara Occidental: Histoire, vie, et culture.* Paris: Karthala, 1993.

Goulding, Marrack. *Peacemonger.* London: John Murray, 2002.

Hodges, Tony. *Western Sahara: The Roots of a Desert War.* Westport, Conn.: Lawrence Hill, 1983.

———. *The Western Saharans.* London: Minority Rights Group, 1984.

International Court of Justice. *Western Sahara.* International Court of Justice, The Hague, 16 October 1975.

Kamil, Leo. *Fueling the Fire: U.S. Policy and the Western Sahara Conflict.* Trenton, N.J.: Red Sea, 1987.

Mercer, John. *The Sahrawis of Western Sahara.* London: Minority Rights Group, 1979.

———. *Spanish Sahara.* London: George Allen and Unwin, 1976.

Perez de Cuellar, Javier. *Pilgrimage for Peace.* New York: St. Martin's, 1997.

Pazzanita, Anthony G. *Western Sahara.* Oxford: Clio, 1996.

Pazzanita, Anthony, and Tony Hodges. *Historical Dictionary of Western Sahara.* London: Scarecrow Press, 1994.

Rezette, Robert. *The Western Sahara and the Frontiers of Morocco.* Paris: Nouvelles Editions Latines, 1975.

Smith de Cherif, Teresa K. "Western Sahara: A Moroccan-Style Election?" *Review of African Political Economy,* no. 58 (November 1993).

United Nations. *Report of the Secretary-General on the Situation Concerning Western Sahara.* Document S/21360, 18 June 1990.

———. Document S/22464, 19 April 1991.

———. Document S/23299, 19 December 1991.

———. Document S/23662, 28 February 1992.

———. Document S/24040, 29 May 1992.

———. Document S/24464, 20 August 1992.

———. Document S/25170, 26 January 1993.

———. Document S/25818, 21 May 1993.

———. Document S/26797, 24 November 1993.

———. Document S/1994/283, 10 March 1994.

———. Document S/1994/819, 12 July 1994.

———. Document S/1994/1257, 5 November 1994.

———. Document S/1995/240, 30 March 1995.

———. Document S/1995/404, 19 May 1995.

———. Document S/1995/779, 8 September 1995.

———. Document S/1995/986, 24 November 1995.

———. Document S/1996/43, 19 January 1996.

———. Document S/1996/343, 8 May 1996.

———. Document S/1996/674, 20 August 1996.

———. Document S/1996/913, 5 November 1996.

———. Document S/1997/166, 27 February 1997.

———. Document S/1997/358, 5 May 1997.

———. Document S/1997/742, 24 September 1997.

———. Document S/1998/35, 15 January 1998.

———. Document S/1998/316, 13 April 1998.

———. Document S/1998/534, 18 June 1998.

———. Document S/1998/634, 10 July 1998.

———. Document S/1998/775, 18 August 1998.

———. Document S/1998/849, 11 September 1998.

———. Document S/1999/88, 28 January 1999.

———. Document S/1999/307, 22 March 1999.

———. Document S/1999/483, 27 April 1999.
———. Document S/1999/483/Add.1, 13 May 1999.
———. Document S/1999/721, 25 June 1999.
———. Document S/1999/1219, 6 December 1999.
———. Document S/2000/131, 17 February 2000.
———. Document S/2000/461, 22 May 2000.
———. Document S/2000/683, 12 July 2000.
———. Document S/2000/1029, 25 October 2000.
———. Document S/2001/148, 20 February 2001.
———. Document S/2001/398, 24 April 2001.
———. Document S/2001/613, 20 June 2001.
———. Document S/2002/41, 10 January 2002.
———. Document S/2002/178, 19 February 2002.
———. Document S/2002/467, 19 April 2002.
———. Document S/2003/59, 16 January 2003.
———. Document S/2003/565, 23 May 2003.
———. Document S/2003/1016, 16 October 2003.
———. Document S/2004/39, 19 January 2004.
———. *Report of the Secretary-General in Pursuance of Security Council Resolution 377 (1975).* Document S/11863, 31 October 1975.
———. *Report of the U.N. Visiting Mission to Spanish Sahara, May-June 1975.* General Assembly Official Records, 30th session, suppl. 23, Document A/10023 Rev 1.
———. Document S/11880, 19 November 1975, Annex III, Security Council Official Records, suppl. for October/November/December.
———. Document S/1995/498, 21 June 1995.
———. Document S/1995/524, 23 June 1995.
———. Document S1995/514, 26 June 1995.
———. Document S/1995/924, 27 October 1995.
———. Document S/2003/1028, 21 October 2003.
———. Document S/2003/1045, 28 October 2003.
———. Resolution of the General Assembly 2072 (XX), 16 December 1965.
———. Resolution of the General Assembly 3458 A, 10 December 1976.
———. Resolution of the General Assembly 3458 B, 10 December 1976.
———. Resolution of the General Assembly 39/40, 5 December 1984.
———. Resolution of the General Assembly 40/50, 2 December 1985.
———. Resolution of the General Assembly 43/33, 22 November 1988.
———. Resolution of the General Assembly 45/266, 17 May 1991.
———. Resolution of the General Assembly 50/36, 6 December 1995.
———. Resolution of the Security Council 621 (1988), 20 September 1988.
———. Resolution of the Security Council 658 (1990), 27 June 1990.
———. Resolution of the Security Council 690 (1991), 29 April 1991.
———. Resolution of the Security Council 725 (1991), 31 December 1991.
———. Resolution of the Security Council 809 (1993), 2 March 1993.
———. Resolution of the Security Council 907 (1994), 29 March 1994.
———. Resolution of the Security Council 1033 (1995), 19 December 1995.
———. Resolution of the Security Council 1042 (1996), 31 January 1996
———. Resolution of the Security Council 1056 (1996), 29 May 1996.
———. Resolution of the Security Council 1263 (1999), 13 September 1999.
———. Resolution of the Security Council 1394 (2002), 27 February 2002.
———. Resolution of the Security Council 1429 (2002), 30 July 2002.

————. Resolution of the Security Council 1495 (2003), 31 July 2003.

————. Resolution of the Security Council 1513 (2003), 28 October 2003.

————. *Yearbook of the United Nations.* New York: United Nations Office of Public Information, 1964–1995.

United Nations High Commissioner for Refugees (UNHCR). *Programme of Humanitarian Assistance in the Tindouf Area.* Document HCR/155/42/76, 1976.

Waldheim, Kurt. *In the Eye of the Storm.* London: Weidenfeld and Nicolson, 1985.

Zartman, I. William. *Ripe for Resolution: Conflict and Intervention in Africa.* New York: Oxford University Press, 1989.

Zoubir, Yahia H. "Origins and Development of the Conflict in Western Sahara." In *International Dimensions of the Western Sahara Conflict,* ed. Yahia H. Zoubir and Daniel Volman. Westport, Conn.: Greenwood, 1993.

————. "Protracted Conflict and Failure to Achieve Prenegotiation in the Western Sahara Conflict." *Humboldt Journal of Social Relations* 20, no. 2 (1994).

Zoubir, Yahia H., and Daniel Volman, eds. *International Dimensions of the Western Sahara Conflict.* Westport, Conn.: Greenwood, 1993.

Index

63; to consider applications from persons claiming the right to participate in referendum, 42; determination of language used in registration forms, 62–63; determination of voting rights, 59–71; establishment of rules of procedure by, 42; Frente Polisario observers on, 40; identification process in, 59; instruction to, 151–157; logistics battalion of, 43; mandate to update previous Spanish census, 42; Moroccan observers on, 40; Organization of African Unity observers on, 40; problem with observer status for Organization of African Unity, 69, 70; procedural details of identification, 68; re-establishment of, 52; registration commencement, 64; role of shaikhs in, 42–43, 65, 66; signals/medical units, 43; staff training, 68; success in launching identification process, 69–71; suspension of process, 87, 88; tribal leaders and, 40. *See also* Voting identification

Ifni, 25

"Instructions relating to the tasks of the Identification Commission," 46

International Court of Justice, 27, 31

Iraq, 110

Islam, 21, 22, 27

Istiqlal, 25

Ivory Coast, 36*n1*

Izarguien tribe, 60

Khadad, Emhamed, 42

Khadiri, General, 55, 65

Kissinger, Henry, 28, 30*n8*

Libya: alliance with Morocco, 33; in Arab Maghreb Union, 36; support for Frente Polisario, 14

Mackenzie, Donald, 23, 24

Madagascar, 30

Madrid Accords (1975), 27, 28, 29, 30*n9*, 31, 107

Mali, 36*n1*

Mansour, Ahmed el, 22

Manz, Johannes, 45, 46

Maqil people, 22

Mauritania, 14, 23; in Arab Maghreb Union, 36; attacks by Frente Polisario, 32; comments on "Peace Plan for Self-Determination of the People of Western Sahara," 17; conflict with Morocco, 25; ends involvement in Western Sahara, 32; identification centers in, 79; military coup in, 32; opening of registration offices in, 67; relinquished control of Western Sahara, 14; trade routes, 24

MINURSO. *See* United Nations Mission for the Referendum in Western Sahara

Mohamed VI (King of Morocco), 18, 107, 110, 113

Morocco, 14, 23; acceptance of controlled referendum, 32; acceptance of framework agreement, 17; "agreement in principle" with United Nations plan, 35; agrees to United Nations supervision of referendum, 34; alliance with Libya, 33; in Arab Maghreb Union, 36; argument on identification process for participation in referendum, 17, 50, 59–71, 76, 79, 84; armed conflict with Frente Polisario, 32; Army of Liberation in, 25; asked by United Nations to negotiate with Frente Polisario, 32; breaking diplomatic relations with Algeria, 31; comments on "Peace Plan for Self-Determination of the People of Western Sahara," 17; commitment to settlement plan, 105; conflict with Mauritania, 25; conquest of, 22; consistency in attitudes on requirements, 13, 50; continued claim to territory, 115; coup attempt in, 26; dealing with Frente Polisario on plan, 51, 52; differences of interpretation with Frente Polisario, 45; direct talks with Frente Polisario, 52–54; framework agreement and, 106–113; gain of Ifni, 26; Green March by, 27, 28, 46; independence from France, 25; integration with, 13; interest in referendum leading to integration, 45, 48; Istiqlal in, 25; jus sanguinis principle for voting entitlement, 13, 92; leaves

About This Publication

The long-running conflict over the sovereignty of Western Sahara has involved all the states of northwest Africa and many beyond since Spain ceded the territory to Morocco and Mauritania in 1976. Erik Jensen traces the evolution of the conflict—from its colonial roots to its present manifestation as a political stalemate.

Jensen reviews the history of the dispute, describes the quest by the UN and interested states to facilitate a process of self-determination through a referendum on independence versus integration with Morocco, and explores the impasse over how to determine who should be allowed to vote in such a referendum. He then turns to the more recent efforts of UN Secretary-General Kofi Annan's personal envoy for Western Sahara, James Baker, to resolve the conflict. Despite Baker's 2003 peace plan, the government of Morocco and the Polisario Front remain at odds, and the stalemate continues.

Erik Jensen served with the UN Mission for the Referendum in Western Sahara (MINURSO) in 1993–1998, from 1994 as head of mission. Since retiring as UN undersecretary general, he has been Warburg Professor of International Relations at Simmons College and visiting fellow at the London School of Economics and Political Science. His recent publications include *Collective Security, Posse, or Global Cop: The US and Global Security at the Turn of the Century*.

The International Peace Academy

The International Peace Academy (IPA) is an independent, international institution dedicated to promoting the prevention and settlement of armed conflicts between and within states through policy research and development.

Founded in 1970, the IPA has built an extensive portfolio of activities in fulfillment of its mission:

- Symposiums, workshops, and other forums that facilitate strategic thinking, policy development, and organizational innovation within international organizations.
- Policy research on multilateral efforts to prevent, mitigate, or rebuild after armed conflict.
- Research, consultations, and technical assistance to support capacities for peacemaking, peacekeeping, and peacebuilding in Africa.
- Professional-development seminars for political, development, military, humanitarian, and nongovernmental personnel involved in peacekeeping and conflict resolution.
- Facilitation in conflict situations where its experience, credibility, and independence can complement official peace efforts.
- Outreach to build public awareness on issues related to peace and security, multilateralism, and the United Nations.

The IPA works closely with the United Nations, regional and other international organizations, governments, and nongovernmental organizations, as well as with parties to conflicts in selected cases. Its efforts are enhanced by its ability to draw on a worldwide network of government and business leaders, scholars, diplomats, military officers, and leaders of civil society.

The IPA is a nonprofit organization governed by an international Board of Directors. The organization is funded by generous donations from governments, major philanthropic foundations, and corporate donors, as well as contributions from individuals and its Board members.

International Peace Academy Publications

Available from Lynne Rienner Publishers, 1800 30th Street, Boulder, Colorado 80301 (303-444-6684), www.rienner.com.

Western Sahara: Anatomy of a Stalemate, Erik Jensen (2005)

Exploring Subregional Conflict: Opportunities for Conflict Prevention, edited by Chandra Lekha Sriram and Zoe Nielsen (2004)

West Africa's Security Challenges: Building Peace in a Troubled Region, edited by Adekeye Adebajo and Ismail Rashid (2004)

War Economies in a Regional Context: Challenges of Transformation, Michael Pugh and Neil Cooper, with Jonathan Goodhand (2004)

The UN Security Council: From the Cold War to the Twenty-First Century, edited by David M. Malone (2004)

The Political Economy of Armed Conflict: Beyond Greed and Grievance, edited by Karen Ballentine and Jake Sherman (2003)

From Promise to Practice: Strengthening UN Capacities for the Prevention of Violent Conflict, edited by Chandra Lekha Sriram and Karin Wermester (2003)

China and India: Cooperation or Conflict? Waheguru Pal Singh Sidhu and Jing-dong Yuan (2003)

The Chittagong Hill Tracts, Bangladesh: On the Difficult Road to Peace, Amena Mohsin (2003)

Peacekeeping in East Timor: The Path to Independence, Michael G. Smith with Moreen Dee (2003)

From Cape to Congo: Southern Africa's Evolving Security Challenges, edited by Mwesiga Baregu and Christopher Landsberg (2003)

Ending Civil Wars: The Implementation of Peace Agreements, edited by Stephen John Stedman, Donald Rothchild, and Elizabeth M. Cousens (2002)

Sanctions and the Search for Security: Challenges to UN Action, David Cortright and George A. Lopez, with Linda Gerber (2002)

Ecuador vs. Peru: Peacemaking Amid Rivalry, Monica Herz and João Pontes Nogueira (2002)

Liberia's Civil War: Nigeria, ECOMOG, and Regional Security in West Africa, Adekeye Adebajo (2002)

Building Peace in West Africa: Liberia, Sierra Leone, and Guinea-Bissau, Adekeye Adebajo (2002)

Kosovo: An Unfinished Peace, William G. O'Neill (2002)

From Reaction to Conflict Prevention: Opportunities for the UN System, edited by Fen Osler Hampson and David M. Malone (2002)

Peacemaking in Rwanda: The Dynamics of Failure, Bruce D. Jones (2001)

Self-Determination in East Timor: The United Nations, the Ballot, and International Intervention, Ian Martin (2001)

Civilians in War, edited by Simon Chesterman (2001)

Toward Peace in Bosnia: Implementing the Dayton Accords, Elizabeth M. Cousens and Charles K. Cater (2001)

Sierra Leone: Diamonds and the Struggle for Democracy, John L. Hirsch (2001)

Peacebuilding as Politics: Cultivating Peace in Fragile Societies, edited by Elizabeth M. Cousens and Chetan Kumar (2001)

The Sanctions Decade: Assessing UN Strategies in the 1990s, David Cortright and George A. Lopez (2000)

Greed and Grievance: Economic Agendas in Civil War, edited by Mats Berdal and David M. Malone (2000)

Building Peace in Haiti, Chetan Kumar (1998)

Rights and Reconciliation: UN Strategies in El Salvador, Ian Johnstone (1995)